编 委

郝文杰	全国民航职业教育教学指导委员会副秘书长、中国民航管理干部学院副教授
江丽容	全国民航职业教育教学指导委员会委员、国际金钥匙学院福州分院院长
林增学	桂林旅游学院旅游学院党委书记
丁永玲	武汉商学院旅游管理学院教授
史金鑫	中国民航大学乘务学院民航空保系主任
刘元超	西南航空职业技术学院空保学院院长
杨文立	上海民航职业技术学院安全员培训中心主任
范月圆	江苏航空职业技术学院航空飞行学院副院长
定 琦	郑州旅游职业学院现代服务学院副院长
黄 华	浙江育英职业技术学院航空学院副院长
王姣蓉	武汉商贸职业学院现代管理技术学院院长
毛颖善	珠海城市职业技术学院旅游管理学院副院长
黄华勇	毕节职业技术学院航空学院副院长
魏 日	江苏旅游职业学院旅游学院副院长
吴 云	上海旅游高等专科学校外语学院院长
刘晏辰	三亚航空旅游职业学院民航空保系主任
田 文	中国民航大学乘务学院民航空保系讲师
汤 黎	武汉职业技术学院旅游与航空服务学院副教授
江 群	武汉职业技术学院旅游与航空服务学院副教授
汪迎春	浙江育英职业技术学院航空学院副教授
段莎琪	张家界航空工业职业技术学院副教授
王勤勤	江苏航空职业技术学院航空飞行学院副教授
覃玲媛	广西蓝天航空职业学院航空管理系主任
付 翠	河北工业职业技术大学空乘系主任
李 岳	青岛黄海学院空乘系主任
王观军	福州职业技术学院空乘系主任
王海燕	新疆职业大学空中乘务系主任
谷建云	湖南女子学院管理学院副教授
牛晓斐	湖南女子学院管理学院讲师

高等职业学校"十四五"规划民航服务类系列教材

民航乘务英语

主　编◎段莎琪
副主编◎付　翠　张　鹏　陈　苇　徐　倩　丁唯也

内 容 提 要

本教材为顺应教学改革要求,探索专业英语模块化教学方式,根据民航客舱服务的职业特点,将内容分为迎送旅客、空中服务、特殊情境、客舱安全和应急,以及着陆 5 个模块,共 16 个单元。这样的编排既符合客舱服务的实际,也有利于教学。每个单元包含听力、客舱服务对话、机上广播词、角色扮演、练习、拓展阅读六个部分,各部分内容长度适宜,具有较强的灵活性和实用性,易于教师教学和学生掌握。

本教材以培养和提高学生英语实际应用能力和客舱服务质量为目标,提供了大量的英语口语训练素材和空中乘务所需的专业知识、专业词汇以及常用句型,使学生能够学以致用,具备现代民航机上服务岗位所需要的基本能力。

图书在版编目(CIP)数据

民航乘务英语/段莎琪主编.—武汉:华中科技大学出版社,2022.9
ISBN 978-7-5680-8772-8

Ⅰ.①民… Ⅱ.①段… Ⅲ.①民用航空-乘务人员-英语 Ⅳ.①F560.9

中国版本图书馆 CIP 数据核字(2022)第 170486 号

民航乘务英语 段莎琪 主编
Minhang Chengwu Yingyu

策划编辑:	胡弘扬 汪 杭
责任编辑:	仇雨亭 陈 然
封面设计:	廖亚萍
责任校对:	张会军
责任监印:	周治超
出版发行:	华中科技大学出版社(中国·武汉) 电话:(027)81321913
	武汉市东湖新技术开发区华工科技园 邮编:430223
录 排:	华中科技大学惠友文印中心
印 刷:	武汉开心印印刷有限公司
开 本:	787mm×1092mm 1/16
印 张:	9.75
字 数:	312 千字
版 次:	2022 年 9 月第 1 版第 1 次印刷
定 价:	42.80 元

本书若有印装质量问题,请向出版社营销中心调换
全国免费服务热线:400-6679-118 竭诚为您服务
版权所有 侵权必究

INTRODUCTION
出版说明

民航业是推动我国经济社会发展的重要战略产业之一。"十四五"时期,我国民航业将进入发展阶段转换期、发展质量提升期、发展格局拓展期。2021年1月在京召开的全国民航工作会议指出,"十四五"期末,我国民航运输规模将再上一个新台阶,通用航空市场需求将进一步激活。这预示着我国民航业将进入更好、更快的发展通道。而我国民航业的快速发展模式,也进一步对我国民航教育和人才培养提出了更高的要求。

2021年3月,民航局印发《关于"十四五"期间深化民航改革工作的意见》,明确了科教创新体系的改革任务,要做到既面向生产一线又面向世界一流。在人才培养过程中,教材建设是重要环节。因此,出版一套把握新时代发展趋势的高水平、高质量的规划教材,是我国民航教育和民航人才建设的重要目标。

基于此,华中科技大学出版社作为教育部直属的重点大学出版社,为深入贯彻习近平总书记对职业教育工作作出的重要指示,助力民航强国战略的实施与推进,特汇聚一大批全国高水平民航院校学科带头人、一线骨干"双师型"教师以及民航领域行业专家等,合力编著高等职业学校"十四五"规划民航服务类系列教材。

本套教材以引领和服务专业发展为宗旨,系统总结民航业实践经验和教学成果,在教材内容和形式上积极创新,具有以下特点:

一、强化课程思政,坚持立德树人

本套教材引入"课程思政"元素,树立素质教育理念,践行当代民航精神,将忠诚担当的政治品格、严谨科学的专业精神等内容贯穿于整个教材,使学生在学习知识的"获得感"中,获得个人前途与国家命运紧密相连的认知,旨在培养德才兼备的民航人才。

二、校企合作编写,理论贯穿实践

本套教材由国内众多民航院校的骨干教师、资深专家学者联合多年从事乘务工作的一线专家共同编写,将最新的企业实践经验和学校教科研理念融入教材,把必要的服务理论和专业能力放在同等重要的位置,以期培养具备行业知识、职业道德、服务理论和服务思想的高层次、高质量人才。

三、内容形式多元化,配套资源立体化

本套教材在内容上强调案例导向、图表教学,将知识系统化、直观化,注重可操作性。华中科技大学出版社同时为本套教材建设了内容全面的线上教材课程资源服务平台,为师生们提供全系列教学计划方案、教学课件、习题库、案例库、教学视频音频等配套教学资源,从而打造线上线下、课内课外的新形态立体化教材。

我国民航业发展前景广阔,民航教育任重道远,为民航事业的发展培养高质量的人才是社会各界的共识与责任。本套教材汇集来自全国的骨干教师和一线专家的智慧与心血,相信其能够为我国民航人才队伍建设、民航高等教育体系优化起到一定的推动作用。

本套教材的编写难免有疏漏、不足之处,恳请各位专家、学者以及广大师生在使用过程中批评指正,以利于教材质量的进一步提高,也希望并诚挚邀请全国民航院校及行业的专家学者加入我们这套教材的编写队伍,共同推动我国民航高等教育事业不断向前发展。

华中科技大学出版社

2021 年 11 月

PREFACE
前言

随着中国航空业的发展,国际航线日益增多,为了提高机上服务水平,尤其是提高空中乘务人员的英语实际应用能力,我们在大量的空中乘务专业英语教学实践的基础上,广泛调研与充分论证,结合实际工作岗位需求,精心编写了《民航乘务英语》这一本教材。本教材针对空中乘务专业编写,以培养和提高学生英语实际应用能力和客舱服务质量为目标。本教材提供了大量的英语口语训练素材和空中乘务所需的专业知识、专业词汇以及常用句型,使学生能够学以致用,具备现代民航机上服务岗位所需要的基本能力。

为顺应教学改革要求,探索专业英语模块化教学方式,根据客舱服务的职业特点,本教材分为迎送旅客、空中服务、特殊情景、客舱安全和应急,以及着陆5个模块,共16个单元,这样的编排既符合客舱服务的实际,也有利于教学。每个单元包含六个部分,各部分内容长度适宜,具有较强的灵活性和实用性,易于教师教学和学生掌握。各部分的内容及功能介绍如下:

第一部分为听力。该部分以民航服务行业为背景,通过原汁原味的客舱对话和有针对性的练习,提高学生的听说能力。

第二部分为客舱服务对话。该部分提供身临其境的职业场景和丰富的民航知识,培养学生的英语交际能力,提高学生的客舱服务水平。本部分是本教材最重要的部分,要求学生熟练掌握。

第三部分为机上广播词。该部分旨在训练学生以标准的语音语调朗读广播词,帮助学生提高英语广播水平和职业素养。该部分是重点,要求学生充分练习。

第四部分为角色扮演。该部分通过设定的情景,要求学生进行口语活动,旨在训练学生在模拟场景中的英语交际能力。

第五部分为练习。该部分练习材料取自真实的职业场景,大量的趣味性、任务型练习能够扩大学生的专业知识面,为学生日后从事航空服务工作打下基础。

第六部分为拓展阅读。该部分取材于国内外航空服务一线岗位的核心内容,详细介绍了乘务员岗位所需的业务能力知识,并精心设计了实用练习,能有效提高学生的民航乘务英语水平和专业技能水平。

本教材共分为16个单元,由段莎琪担任主编。第1、10、13、14单元由段莎琪编写;第4、7、8单元由付翠编写;第9、11、12单元由张鹏编写;第2、3单元由陈苇编写;第5、6单元由徐倩编写;第15、16单元由丁唯也编写。段莎琪负责全书统稿工作。

本教材在编写过程中得到了张家界航空工业职业技术学院、河北工业职业技术大学、山东女子学院、广西蓝天航空职业学院、武汉商贸职业学院、江苏旅游职业学院各位老师和领导的大力支持和帮助,在此表示衷心感谢! 由于编者时间紧、水平有限,书中难免存在疏漏和不妥之处,恳请广大读者不吝赐教,提出宝贵意见,再次致以诚挚的谢意!

编者

2022年8月

"民航服务英语"MOOC课程

注:扫描二维码可加入省级精品课程"民航服务英语"学习。

Module 1	**Boarding** ·· 1
	Unit 1 Boarding and Greeting Passengers ············· 1
	Unit 2 Seat Arrangement ······································· 10
	Unit 3 Baggage Arrangement ································· 17
	Unit 4 Safety Check ··· 25

Module 2	**In-flight Service** ··· 32
	Unit 5 Beverage and Meal Service ························· 32
	Unit 6 In-flight Entertainment Service ··················· 39
	Unit 7 Medical Service ··· 45
	Unit 8 Duty-free Service ······································· 51

Module 3	**Special Situation** ··· 59
	Unit 9 Serving Special Passengers ························· 59
	Unit 10 Lost Baggage ··· 67
	Unit 11 Flight Delay ··· 77
	Unit 12 Entry Forms and Transfer ··························· 85

Module 4	**Emergency Situation** ··· 95
	Unit 13 First Aid ··· 95
	Unit 14 Emergency Procedures ······························· 105

Module 5	**Landing** ··· 117
	Unit 15 Pre-arrival ··· 117
	Unit 16 Landing and Farewell ································· 126

附录 A　世界各国主要航空公司代码 ………………………………………………… 135
附录 B　世界主要城市及三字代码 …………………………………………………… 137
附录 C　国内主要城市航空三字代码及机场 ………………………………………… 140
附录 D　机上特殊餐食及代码 ………………………………………………………… 143

Module 1　Boarding

Unit 1　Boarding and Greeting Passengers

Learning Objectives

1. Be familiar with various boarding dialogues and announcements.
2. Grasp relevant English expressions.
3. Know how to arrange seats and baggage.
4. Know the cabin attendants' responsibilities.

Part One　Listening

1 Listen to the dialogue and choose the best answer to each question

(1) Where's the passenger's seat?
A. In the front of the cabin
B. In the middle of the cabin
C. In the back of the cabin

(2) What kind of seat is it?
A. It's an aisle seat.
B. It's a middle seat.
C. It's a window seat.

听力音频

2 Listen to the dialogue and fill in the blanks

(A cabin attendant is welcoming passengers on board.)
CA: cabin attendant　PAX: passenger
CA: Good morning, sir. ＿＿＿(1)＿＿＿!
PAX: Good morning. I can't find my seat.
CA: May ＿＿＿(2)＿＿＿?

PAX: Of course. Here you are.

CA: Your seat number is 4C. Please _____(3)_____ .

PAX: Where is the number?

CA: Your seat number is indicated on the _____(4)_____ .

PAX: Oh, I see. Thank you very much.

CA: My pleasure, sir. If _____(5)_____ .

Part two　Dialogues

CA: cabin attendant　　PAX: passenger

1 Dialogue 1

(A passenger is boarding.)

CA: Good morning, madam. Welcome on board.

PAX: Good morning.

CA: Would you please show me your boarding pass?

PAX: Of course. Here you are.

CA: 15F. It's in the middle of the cabin, the window seat. This way please, I'll show you your seat. Your seat number is indicated on the overhead compartment.

PAX: Thank you.

2 Dialogue 2

PAX1: Excuse me.

CA: Yes? What can I do for you?

PAX1: Could you help me with my seat?

CA: No problem. Your boarding pass, please?

PAX1: Here you are.

CA: Row 18, seat A. Thank you. Just follow me, please.

PAX: Thanks.

(The seat has been occupied by a man.)

CA: Excuse me, sir. I'm afraid you may have taken the wrong seat. May I see your boarding pass?

PAX2: OK. Here you are.

CA: Thank you, sir. I'm afraid you are in the wrong seat. This is 18A, but your seat number is 8A. In the front of the cabin. The number is indicated along the edge of the overhead compartment.

PAX2: Sorry, I'll move, then.

CA: That's all right. May I help you with your baggage.

PAX2: No, Thank you. I can do it myself.

CA: (to PAX1) Sorry to keep you waiting, sir.

PAX1: What a relief! Thank you so much.

CA: You are welcome.

3 Dialogue 3

(A passenger stands in the aisle.)

CA: Excuse me, sir. Could you step aside, please? It can be difficult for others to pass.

PAX: Oh, sorry. But I need to lift my baggage into the locker.

CA: Let me help you.

PAX: Many thanks.

CA: It's my pleasure. This is call button. If there is anything we can do for you, please feel free to let us know. We'll be very glad to serve you.

PAX: Sure. Oh, it's cold here. I feel the wind is blowing over my head.

CA: The service unit is above your head. This is the ventilation adjuster. You can shut it off by turning it tightly to the right.

PAX: I see. Let me try. It's much better now.

CA: Here is the reading light. You can turn it on or off with the button on the unit.

PAX: Good. I like to read during the flight.

4 Dialogue 4

(To a passenger who takes a baby.)

CA: Hello, madam. Welcome on board.

PAX: Thank you.

CA: How old is your baby?

PAX: She'll be 10 months old next week.

CA: She's beautiful. Has she flown before?

PAX: No. This is my first flight with her. I'm hoping she'll stay asleep during the take-off.

CA: OK. Your baby will need to be seated on your lap for take-off and landing. You need to fasten her to your seat belt with a special baby belt. It's just like an extension belt. I'll go and get one for you.

PAX: Thank you.

5 Dialogue 5

CA: Welcome aboard, sir. I'm Fiona. The chief attendant of this flight. If there is anything I can do for you, just let me know. Which class are you flying?

PAX: My ticket says it's business class.

CA: OK. The business class is in the front of the cabin. Just go straight and you will find the business class.

PAX: Where can I sit exactly?

CA: May I see your boarding pass, please?

PAX：Here you are.

CA：Your seat number is 4C. It's an aisle seat.

PAX：I want to change seat. Could you help me with that?

CA：Please follow me. Let's go to the business class and I'll see if there is someone who wants to change seat with you. Is that OK?

PAX：That's very kind of you.

6 Words and expressions

board B［bɔːd］/A［bɔːrd］ v. 登船/飞机 n. 木板
boarding pass 登机牌
overhead compartment 头顶上方行李架
baggage［'bægɪdʒ］n. 手提行李
relief［rɪ'liːf］n. 宽慰；轻松；解脱
aside［ə'saɪd］adv. 到旁边；在旁边
lift［lɪft］v. 举起；抬高 n. 电梯；搭便车
call button 呼叫按钮
blow B［bləʊ］/A［bloʊ］v. 吹；风吹；擤（鼻子）；（保险丝）熔断 n. 打击；猛击
ventilation［ˌventɪ'leɪʃn］n. 通风井
adjuster［ə'dʒʌstə］n. 调节器
fasten B［'fɑːsn］/A［'fæsn］v. 系牢；扣紧；使固定
seat belt 安全带
extension［ɪk'stenʃn］n. 延长；伸展；延期
注：B 为英式读音，A 为美式读音，全书同。

7 Notes to the dialogues

(1) Your seat number is indicated on the overhead compartment.
您的座位号在头顶上方的行李架上。

(2) The seat has been occupied by a man.
那个座位被一位男士占用了。

(3) What a relief!
总算松了一口气。

(4) Here is the reading light. You can turn it on or off with the button on the unit.
这是阅读灯。您可以通过这个按钮来打开或关闭它。

Part Three   Announcements

1 Greeting

Ladies and gentlemen,

Welcome on board Flight CA368 to London. Today our flying time to London will be

广播音频

9 hours and 45 minutes. We'll be cruising at an altitude of 10000 meters. As we'll be crossing the International Date Line, we'll arrive in London today, September 14 at 8:30 local time. If there's anything we can do to make your flight more comfortable, please don't hesitate to let us know.

2 Boarding

Good morning everyone, welcome to NH752 to Paris. My name's Alice. I'm your purser in charge of today's flight. I'd like to introduce our cabin attendants: Lily White is going to be in charge of first class today and Rebecca Ferguson is in charge of economy class. We hope you enjoy the flight.

3 Arrangement

Ladies and gentlemen,

Welcome aboard Hainan Airlines' flight from Changsha to Sanya. Please take your seat according to your seat number. Your seat number is on the edge of the overhead compartment. Please make sure your hand baggage is stored in the overhead compartment. You can put small articles under the seat in front of you. Please take your seat as soon as possible to keep the aisle clear for others to go through.

4 ID check

Ladies and gentlemen,

May I have your attention, please?

The immigration and customs officers need to recheck your boarding passes and passports. Please return to your assigned seats and present the officers with your passports and boarding passes.

Thank you for your cooperation.

5 Words and phrases

cruising [ˈkruːzɪŋ] n. 巡航

altitude B[ˈæltɪtjuːd]/A[ˈæltɪtuːd] n. 海拔

hesitate [ˈhezɪteɪt] v. 犹豫

purser B[ˈpɜːsə(r)]/A[ˈpɜːrsə(r)] n. 乘务长

articles B[ˈɑːtɪklz]/A[ˈɑːrtɪkl] n. pl. 文章；物件

go through 通过

immigration [ˌɪmɪˈɡreɪʃən] n. 移居；移民人数

customs [ˈkʌstəmz] n. 海关

present [ˈpreznt] v. 呈现；展示

International Date Line 国际日期变更线

in charge of 负责；主管

cabin attendant 客舱乘务员

assigned seat 指定座位

cooperation B[kəʊˌɒpəˈreɪʃn]/A [koʊˌɑpəˈreɪʃn] *n.* 合作；协作

6 Notes to the announcements

(1) We'll be cruising at an altitude of 10000 meters.

我们将巡航在一万米高度。

(2) Please take your seat as soon as possible to keep the aisle clear for others to go through.

请尽快找到您的座位，以便其他的旅客顺利通过过道。

(3) Please return to your assigned seats and present the officers with your passports and boarding passes.

请回到您的指定位置，并将您的护照和登机牌出示给工作人员。

Part Four　Role Play

In small groups, make up a dialogue based on the following situations

(1) Passengers A is travelling with her 80-year-old grandmother. Help them find their seats.

(2) Passenger B feels terrible. She needs some hot water.

Part Five　Exercise

1 Fill in the blanks in the following dialogues

Dialogue 1

CA：Good morning, sir. ＿＿＿＿＿＿（1）＿＿＿＿＿＿（欢迎登机）！

PAX：Good morning! ＿＿＿＿＿（2）＿＿＿＿＿（能帮我找一下座位吗）？

CA：Sure. ＿＿＿＿＿（3）＿＿＿＿＿（能给我看下您的登机牌吗，先生）？

PAX：Of course. Here it is.

CA：Thank you. Your seat number is 12A. It's in the ＿＿＿＿＿（4）＿＿＿＿＿（客舱后部），＿＿＿＿＿（5）＿＿＿＿＿（靠窗的座位），＿＿＿＿＿（6）＿＿＿＿＿（请跟我来）.

PAX：Thank you.

Dialogue 2

CA：Good morning, sir. ＿＿＿＿＿（7）＿＿＿＿＿（欢迎登机）！

PAX：Good morning! I can't find my seat.

CA：May ＿＿＿＿＿（8）＿＿＿＿＿（能给我看一下您的登机牌吗，先生）？

PAX：Of course. Here you are.

CA：Your seat number is 4C.

PAX：Where is the number?
CA：You'll see ＿＿＿＿＿（9）＿＿＿＿＿（您的座位号显示在头顶上方行李架边缘处）.
PAX：Oh，I see. Thanks so much.
CA：You are welcome. If ＿＿＿＿＿（10）＿＿＿＿＿（需要帮助的话，请按呼叫按钮）.

2 Translate the following phrases into English

（1）登机牌　　　　　　　　　（2）座位号
（3）头顶上方行李架　　　　　（4）手提行李
（5）呼叫按钮　　　　　　　　（6）随身物品
（7）婴儿安全带　　　　　　　（8）过道
（9）靠窗的座位　　　　　　　（10）经济舱

3 Translate the following sentences into English

（1）请出示您的登机牌。
（2）座位号在头顶上方的行李架上。
（3）请您侧身到一边。
（4）如果您在飞行期间有任何需要，请告诉我。
（5）在起飞和降落时，请将您的安全带系好。

4 Translate the following sentences into Chinese

（1）We'll be cruising at an altitude of 10000 meters.
（2）If there's anything we can do to make your flight more comfortable，please don't hesitate to let us know.
（3）I'm your purser in charge of today's flight.
（4）Please remain in your seat as we expect to depart soon.
（5）Please return to your assigned seats and present the officers with your passports and boarding passes.

5 Read the following things the cabin attendants should do and classify them according to the hint

（1）Make sure the aircraft safety instruction cards are in the back of the passenger seats.
（2）Help passengers put their luggage into the overhead compartment.
（3）Check the toilet.
（4）Arrange passengers to their seats.
（5）Check whether your uniform is clean.
（6）Greeting passengers.
（7）Hand out the arrival immigration forms to complete.
（8）Give special attention to older passengers.
（9）Ask the children not to leave their seats.

(10) Make sure everyone has a blanket.

(11) Check the number of meals.

(12) Make coffee for the passengers.

Before passengers come on board:	When passengers are boarding:

Part Six Supplementary Reading

Flight Crew

Flight crew is a group of people employed by an airline who have duties on board. It consists of two kinds of people: those who are responsible for the safety and efficient operation of an aircraft and those who are responsible for the safety and wellbeing of the passengers on a flight. The first kind of people are called pilots and the other is called cabin crew.

Pilots exercise command over the crew, including the co-pilots (first officers) and cabin crew. An aircraft is usually operated by two, three or four pilots, depending on the type of aircraft and length of the journey. The pilot who is called the captain is the more senior one. He has full responsibility for the safety of the aircraft and its occupants.

Pilots are needed in four areas: passenger scheduled services, passenger charter services, flight services and business aviation (general aviation). Business aviation is the biggest sector worldwide and includes private aircraft, flying schools and companies transporting oil and gas workers to offshore rigs.

Many consider flying to be a dream job but perhaps they have an unrealistic idea about what it is really like. In fact, the job demands a great deal of personal commitment (承诺) and self-sacrifice. A pilot has to pass stringent training courses, and then be tested in recurrent training twice a year in order to maintain the relevant license.

Cabin crew is the people who are working with the passengers in the cabin. They attend to passengers' needs throughout the flight, serving refreshments and selling duty-free goods. So customer service is vital. They are expected to be friendly, enthusiastic and courteous at all times. Cabin crew can also be divided into two groups: the senior member is called flight director or purser and those who work under the senior member are called cabin attendants.

A qualified cabin crew must be with lofty goals and passion. But that's not enough. High level of professionalism and hard working attitude are a must. Language is also important, and an excellent cabin crew must be able to communicate with passengers who do not share the same language in English fluently.

Cabin attendants should carry out a range of duties:

• Attending a pre-flight briefing and crew members are assigned their tasks for the coming flight.

• Carrying out pre-flight duties, including checking the safety equipment, ensuring the aircraft is clean and tidy, ensuring that information in the seat pockets is up to date and that all the meals and sufficient supplies are on board.

• Welcoming passengers on board and directing them to their seats.

• Demonstrating safety procedures and ensuring that all hand baggage is securely stored.

• Checking all passengers' seat belts are secure before take-off.

• Making announcements on behalf of the pilot and answering passengers' questions during the flight.

• Serving meals and refreshments to passengers.

• Selling duty-free goods and informing passengers of any allowance restrictions in force at their destination.

• Reassuring passengers and ensuring that they follow safety procedures correctly in emergency situations.

• Giving first aid to passengers when necessary.

• Ensuring passengers disembark safely at the end of a flight.

• Completing paperwork, including writing a flight report.

The work of cabin attendants can be stressful and demanding, but it can also be a varied, interesting and rewarding role.

Decide the following statements are true (T) or false (F) according to the passage

(1) The people who are responsible for the flying of an aircraft are called flight crew. Pilots exercise command over the captain. (   )

(2) Among the four areas pilots are being needed, general aviation occupied the biggest section. (   )

(3) A pilot has to pass some training courses, and then be tested in recurrent training every two years in order to maintain the relevant license. (   )

(4) Lofty goals and passion are enough for a qualified cabin crew. (   )

(5) Pilots are the people who are working with the passengers in the cabin. (   )

Unit 2　Seat Arrangement

 Learning Objectives

1. Be familiar with various seat arrangement dialogues and announcements.
2. Grasp relevant English expressions.
3. Know how to arrange seats on board.
4. Know about seat arrangement.

Part One　Listening

1　Write down what you hear in the recording

(1) _____　(2) _____　(3) _____
(4) _____　(5) _____　(6) _____
(7) _____　(8) _____　(9) _____
(10) _____

2　Listen to the dialogue and choose the best answer to each question

(1) What mistake has the man made?
A. He hasn't taken a seat.
B. He has taken a wrong seat.
C. He hasn't checked his seat number.

(2) What is the man's seat number?
A. It's 1A.
B. It's 11A.
C. It's not mentioned.

Part Two　Dialogues

CA：cabin attendant　　PAX：passenger

1 Dialogue 1

CA: Good morning, sir. What can I do for you?

PAX: Good morning. I can't find my seat. My boarding pass says it is 30J.

CA: It's in the back of the cabin. This way, please. I'll direct you to your seat.

PAX: OK.

CA: Here is your seat. The seat number is shown on the edge of the overhead compartment. May I help you with your baggage?

PAX: No, thank you.

2 Dialogue 2

(An old lady is boarding.)

CA: Welcome aboard. Let me help you with your baggage and direct you to your seat.

PAX: Thank you. Is my seat an aisle one? I'd like to check it again because taking an aisle seat will make it more convenient for me to go to the toilet during the flight.

CA: Don't worry. Your seat number is 10C, an aisle one. Here is your seat. Please be seated. Where do you want your baggage to be placed? In the overhead compartment or under the seat in front of you?

PAX: I'd like to place it under the seat in front of me.

CA: Let me help you fasten your seat belt. We need to place the metal tip into the buckle and pull on the loose end to tighten the belt. If you want to unfasten the belt, simply release the top of the buckle like this.

PAX: Thank you very much.

CA: The blue button above your head is a call button. If you need any help, please press the button to call us. We'll be very glad to serve you.

PAX: Thanks again. That's very kind of you.

3 Dialogue 3

CA: Good morning, sir.

PAX: Good morning.

CA: According to the safety instructions, the passenger who takes the seat by the emergency exit should help the cabin attendant to open the cabin door here and to evacuate the passengers in the event of emergency. Since you are seated by the emergency exit, are you willing and able to assist with the operation of the exit if necessary?

PAX: Er... No.

CA: It doesn't matter. I'll find another seat for you.

4 Dialogue 4

(Two passengers encounter on the aisle.)

PAX1: Hey! Alice. I didn't expect to meet you here on board.

PAX2: Either did I. Small world, isn't it?

PAX1: I'm so happy to meet you here.

PAX2: So am I. We haven't met each other for several months. I miss you very much. By the way, my assigned seat is 25J. What about you?

PAX1: Mine is 28A. Let's ask the flight attendant to change seats for us. I can't wait to chat with you.

(A cabin attendant is coming toward them.)

PAX1: Hello, I want to sit together with my friend. Our seat numbers are 25J and 28A. Would you please give us a hand?

CA: I see. Just wait for a moment, please.

(The cabin attendant comes to the passenger in 25K.)

CA: Excuse me, Miss. The lady in 28A would like to change her seat with you because her friend takes the seat next to you. Do you mind changing your seat with her?

PAX3: I'm afraid I do. I have already put my baggage in the compartment and I don't want to change my seat.

CA: OK. I see.

(The cabin attendant comes to the passenger in 28B.)

CA: Excuse me, sir. The lady in 25J would like to change her seat with you because her friend takes the seat next to you. Do you mind changing your seat with her.

PAX4: 25J? Let me see. Is it also a middle seat?

CA: No, it's an aisle seat.

PAX4: OK, I like aisle seats. I can change my seat with her.

CA: Thank you.

(The cabin attendant turns to PAX1 and PAX2.)

CA: The passenger in 28B is willing to change his seat with you. Now you can sit together.

PAX1 & PAX 2: Thanks a lot.

CA: My pleasure. If there's anything we can do to make your flight more comfortable, please don't hesitate to let us know.

5 Dialogue 5

PAX: Excuse me, may I take another seat in the rear of the cabin? I find that there is a vacant window seat.

CA: In fact, in order to ensure proper weight and balance for the aircraft when it takes off, passengers are required to be seated in the assigned seats. I'll direct you to the seat as soon as I make sure it's available after take-off.

PAX: Thank you very much.

6 Words and expressions

edge [edʒ] *n.* 边；边缘

buckle ['bʌkl] *v.* (使)搭扣扣住 *n.* (皮带等的)搭扣，锁扣

release [rɪ'liːs] *v.* 释放；松开

emergency exit 紧急出口
evacuate [ɪˈvækjueɪt] v.（把人从危险的地方）疏散，转移
assist [əˈsɪst] v. 帮助；援助
rear B[rɪə(r)]/A[rɪr] n. 后部
vacant [ˈveɪkənt] adj. 空着的；未被占用的
available [əˈveɪləbl] adj. 有空的；可获得的

7　Notes to the dialogues

（1）Please be seated.
请坐。
（2）We need to place the metal tip into the buckle and pull on the loose end to tighten the belt.
我们要把金属片扣入锁扣，拉紧带子。
（3）If you want to unfasten the belt, simply release the top of the buckle like this.
如果您想要解开安全带，像这样将金属扣向外打开即可。
（4）In fact, in order to ensure proper weight and balance for the aircraft when it takes off, passengers are required to be seated in the assigned seats.
实际上，为了保证起飞时飞机的重量和平衡，旅客必须在指定座位上坐好。

Part Three　Announcements

1　Seat arrangement

Good morning, ladies and gentlemen. Welcome aboard China Eastern Airlines. As soon as you enter the cabin, please take your seat according to your seat number. Your seat number is shown on the edge of your overhead compartment. If you can't find your seat, please feel free to ask us.

广播音频

2　Aircraft balance

Ladies and gentlemen,

Welcome aboard! In order to ensure proper weight and balance for the aircraft when it takes off, passengers are required to be seated in the assigned seats. If you really need to change your seat, please ask us to arrange a seat for you. Thank you for your understanding and cooperation.

3　The seat by the emergency exit

Good morning, everyone. Thank you for choosing Air China. If you are taking the seat at an emergency exit, please read the responsibility for emergency exit seating on the safety instructions card which is in your seat pocket. If you are unable to perform these functions, please let us know. We will be happy to find you another seat. Thank you!

4 Recounting passengers

Ladies and gentlemen,

May I have your attention, please?

Now we are going to recount the passengers. Please remain seated in your seat. Passengers who are using the lavatories please return to your assigned seat.

Thank you for your cooperation.

5 Words and phrases

perform B[pəˈfɔːm]/A[pərˈfɔːrm] *v.* 履行；执行；演出

lavatory B[ˈlævətri]/A[ˈlævətɔːri] *n.* 厕所；卫生间

Part Four   Role Play

In small groups, make up a dialogue based on the following situations

(1) Direct a man to his seat in first class.

(2) A little girl is travelling alone. Help her to find her seat.

Part Five   Exercise

1 Translate the following phrases into English

(1) 指定的座位   (2) 中间的座位

(3) 靠走道的座位   (4) 头等舱

(5) 座位安排   (6) 商务舱

(7) 在机舱尾部   (8) 空的座位

(9) 洗手间   (10) 起飞

(11) 挨着   (12) 解开安全带

2 Translate the following sentences into English

(1) 这是您的座位。

(2) 我带您去您的座位。

(3) 我给您换个座位。

(4) 25B 的乘客愿意与您交换座位。

(5) 有一个靠窗的座位是空的。

(6) 请您在座位上坐好。

3 Translate the following sentences into Chinese

(1) Your seat number is 10C.

(2) Is my seat an aisle one?

(3) Please be seated.

(4) Do you mind changing your seat with her?

(5) May I take another seat in the rear of the cabin?

(6) As soon as you enter the cabin, please take your seat according to your seat number as soon as possible.

4 Fill in the blanks in the following dialogues

Dialogue 1

CA: Good afternoon, madam. _____(1)_____ （请问有什么可以帮您）?

PAX: Good morning! _____(2)_____ （能帮我找一下我的座位吗）? _____(3)_____ （这是我的登机牌）.

CA: OK. Your seat number is 20J. _____(4)_____ （这边请）.

PAX: Thank you.

CA: Here is your seat. _____(5)_____ （座位号在头顶行李架边缘）.

PAX: Got it.

CA: _____(6)_____ （需要我帮您放行李吗）?

PAX: No, thanks. _____(7)_____ （我自己来吧）.

Dialogue 2

CA: Excuse me, sir. _____(8)_____ （您介意和10排的一位女士交换一下座位吗）?

PAX: Which row?

CA: Row 10. It's 10A.

PAX: _____(9)_____ （她的座位也是靠走道的座位吗）?

CA: No, _____(10)_____ （是靠窗的座位）.

PAX: I like window seat. _____(11)_____ （我可以和她交换位子）.

CA: Thank you. _____(12)_____ （我带您去她的座位）.

5 Write an announcement and practise reading your announcement

Write an announcement about seat arrangement requirements for proper weight and balance of the aircraft and for the emergency exit seating. Flight information is listed as follows.

Airline: China Eastern Airlines

Flight number: MU 568

From: Shanghai

To: Beijing

Part Six   Supplementary Reading

Seat Arrangement on Board

  As it's known to all, check-in is an important part before boarding the plane and passengers can choose their seats when checking in. Nowadays, technology allows people to check in online which offers a clear picture for people to see which seat they can choose. Passengers seem to choose the seats according to their wishes, but in fact, they are still under the control of the airlines.

  To ensure a safe flight, the aircraft should keep proper balance. Every object has a center of gravity, and so does an aircraft. To keep proper balance of an aircraft means to make the aircraft's center of gravity within a safe range. Seat arrangement on board is among the factors determining the aircraft's center of gravity. Then how to control the seat arrangement?

  In fact, there is a position called loading and balance personnel, one of his jobs is to monitor passengers' selection of aircraft seats at all times during checkin. The loading and balance personnel are required to lock the seats on the system according to the balance characteristics of various types of aircraft. When the aircraft's center of gravity is in the front, the loading and balance personnel lock the seats in the front rows of the aircraft and release the seats in the back. When the center of gravity of the aircraft is in the back, the loading and balance personnel then lock the seats in the back and release the seats in the front. When there aren't many passengers, it is necessary to accurately control and lock the seats in a large area. Aircraft's center of gravity changes with the arrangement of passenger seats, that's why the loading and balance personnel must monitor the selection of aircraft seats at all times, and control the seat arrangement according to the change of aircraft's center of gravity.

  As long as a seat is locked on the system, passengers can't select the seat. Besides, once selected, the seat is the assigned seat for the passenger. For the safety of the entire flight, passengers had better not change their seats at will. Changing seats in a large area will change the position of the aircraft's center of gravity and then change the aircraft's balance, which will seriously affect flight safety. This doesn't mean passengers can't change their seats at all. If passengers feel uncomfortable or there are vacant seats on board, they can ask cabin attendants for rearrangement and the cabin attendants will decide whether to rearrange the seats according to the safety regulations. Besides, one case should be paid great attention. If passengers take the seats by the emergency exits, they should be sure that they can assist the cabin attendants in case of emergency, including opening the cabin door, assisting other passengers to escape and so on. Accordingly, if the passengers of this row can't perform these functions, they can ask the cabin attendants to rearrange them.

Decide the following statements are true (T) or false (F) according to the passage

(1) Passengers can only check in at the airport. (   )

(2) Seat arrangement on board can affect the aircraft's center of gravity. (   )

(3) Loading and balance personnel should monitor passengers' selection of aircraft seats at all times during the entire flight. (   )

(4) Passengers can change their seats as they wish during the flight. (   )

(5) If there are vacant seats in the cabin, passengers can take the vacant seats. (   )

(6) If the passengers sitting by the emergency exits are unable to assist the cabin attendants in case of emergency, they can ask the cabin attendants to find other seats for them. (   )

Unit 3   Baggage Arrangement

Learning Objectives

1. Be familiar with various baggage arrangement dialogues and announcements.
2. Grasp relevant English expressions.
3. Know how to arrange baggage.
4. Know about baggage service.

Part One   Listening

1 Listen to the dialogue and choose the best answer to each question

(1) Why doesn't the passenger know where to store her backpack?

A. Because there is no room for her backpack.

B. Because this is her first time traveling by air.

C. Because it's too heavy for her to store her backpack by herself.

(2) Where can't the woman store her backpack?

A. In the overhead compartment

B. On the seat

C. Under the seat in front of her

听力音频

2 Listen to the dialogue and fill in the blanks

CA: cabin attendant   PAX: passenger

CA: Excuse me, madam? _____(1)_____?

PAX: Yes.

CA: I'm afraid you can't leave your suitcase _____(2)_____. You can store it _____(3)_____.

PAX: Um, there is little room for my suitcase and I've also tried to put it under the seat in front of me, but _____(4)_____.

CA: Well, _____(5)_____. The overhead compartment in the rear cabin is available. If you don't mind, _____(6)_____.

PAX: _____(7)_____. Thank you.

CA: You are welcome.

Part Two   Dialogues

CA: cabin attendant   PAX: passenger

1 Dialogue 1

CA: Welcome aboard, Miss. Would you like me to help you with your baggage?

PAX: Ah, yes! Actually I'm going crazy with my baggage.

CA: Take it easy. The baggage is usually stored in the overhead compartment or under the seat in front of you. Let me see. (The cabin attendant opens the overhead compartment.) There's still room for your suitcase.

(The cabin attendant helps the passenger place her suitcase into the overhead compartment.)

PAX: The compartment is full now. Um... I can put my bag under the seat. Then how about my coat?

CA: If you don't mind, I would like to hang it in the wardrobe compartment for you.

PAX: Of course not.

CA: Are there any valuable items in your coat?

PAX: No, there aren't. It's so considerate of you. Wow, what a relief now!

CA: Is there anything else I can do for you?

PAX: No. Thanks very much. You've helped me a lot.

CA: With pleasure. Don't hesitate to ask me if you have any problems.

PAX: OK. Thanks again.

2 Dialogue 2

(A passenger is sitting at an aisle seat holding a backpack in her arms.)

CA: Excuse me, madam. Would you like me to help you stow your backpack in your overhead compartment?

PAX: No, thanks. I want to keep it in my sight.

CA: Well, how about placing it under the seat in front of you?

PAX: I'll have no legroom for the entire flight. I can hold it in my arms.

CA: I'm afraid you can't do that, because it will cause trouble for other passengers in your row and it is dangerous in case of turbulence.

PAX: OK. I'll place it into the overhead compartment.

CA: If you like, I can place it for you.

PAX: No, thanks. I can do it myself.

3 Dialogue 3

CA: Excuse me, sir. I'm afraid you can't leave your baggage by the emergency exit.

PAX: Oh, I'm sorry, but the overhead compartment is so full that I can hardly put my bag into it and I don't want to leave my bag under the seat, because I want more legroom to relax.

CA: Actually, passengers who take seats in the emergency exit row can't place the baggage by the emergency exit or under the seat. Since your overhead compartment is full, would you like to leave your bag with me? I'll look after it for you with care.

PAX: OK. Many thanks.

CA: It's my pleasure.

4 Dialogue 4

CA: Hello, may I help you with your baggage?

PAX: Actually I don't know where to place my stroller.

CA: Is it a collapsible one?

PAX: Yes, it is.

CA: Well, let me fold your stroller and put it into your overhead compartment.

PAX: It's so nice of you. Thank you.

CA: You are welcome. What's more, the call button is above your head. If you need help, don't hesitate to contact me.

PAX: OK.

5 Dialogue 5

PAX: Excuse me. Can you do me a favor?

CA: Yes, sir. What can I do for you?

PAX: I have a vase with me and I don't know how to stow it on board.

CA: May I have your boarding pass, please?

PAX: Here you are.

CA: Let me see. Your seat number is 46J and you have an extra seat 46K for your vase.

This way, please.

(The passenger follows the cabin attendant to his seat.)

CA: The seat number is shown on the edge of the overhead compartment. You have a middle seat and your vase should be placed on the window seat next to you. Now let me help you with your baggage.

PAX: OK.

(The cabin attendant assists the man in placing the vase.)

CA: Let me fasten the seat belt for your vase. Please don't loosen the seat belt until the plane stops completely. Moreover, since your vase is fragile and valuable, please take good care of it during the flight.

PAX: OK. I see.

CA: How about your backpack? Would you like to place it under the seat in front of you or in your overhead compartment?

PAX: I'd like to put it under the seat and I'll do it myself. Thanks for helping me.

CA: It's my pleasure.

6 Words and expressions

wardrobe B ['wɔːdrəʊb] /A ['wɔːrdroʊb] n. 衣柜；衣橱

backpack ['bækpæk] n. 背包

stow B [stəʊ]/A [stoʊ] v. 储藏；收藏

turbulence B ['tɜːbjələns] /A ['tɜrbjələns] n. 颠簸；湍流；混乱

stroller B ['strəʊlə(r)]/A ['stroʊlə(r)] n. 婴儿推车

collapsible [kə'læpsəbl] adj. 可折叠的

fold B [fəʊld]/ A[foʊld] v. 折叠

vase B [vɑːz]/A [veɪs] n. 瓶；花瓶

extra seat 占座座位

fragile B ['frædʒaɪl]/A ['frædʒl] adj. 易碎的

7 Notes to the dialogues

(1) Take it easy.

别着急。放轻松。

(2) The baggage is usually stored in the overhead compartment or under the seat in front of you.

行李通常放在头顶上方的行李架或者前方座椅的下面。

(3) It's so considerate of you.

你真是太贴心了。

(4) extra seat

占座座位

旅客可以为超过手提行李限额但是需要带进客舱的行李购买座位，以放置并运送行李。可以购买客舱占座行李票的行李主要为乐器、神像、精密仪器、电器等贵重或易碎物品。

Part Three　Announcements

1　After entering the cabin

Good morning, ladies and gentlemen. Thank you for taking Air China. As you enter the cabin, please take your seat as soon as possible. Your baggage can be stowed in the overhead compartment or under the seat in front of you. According to the safety instructions, the baggage can't be placed on the aisle or by the emergency exits. If you need any help, please feel free to let us know. We will be sincerely at your service. Thank you.

2　Before taking off

Ladies and gentlemen,

Welcome aboard China Southern Airlines. Our plane will take off soon. Please check again that your carry-on baggage has been stowed in the overhead compartment or under the seat in front of you. The captain has turned on the Fasten Seat Belt Sign, please fasten your seat belt, open the window shade and make sure your seat back and tray table are in the full upright position. Thank you for your cooperation and we wish you a pleasant flight.

3　During the flight

Ladies and gentlemen,

May I have your attention, please? According to the safety instructions, please don't open the overhead compartment in the case of taxiing, taking off, turbulence and landing. Thank you for your understanding and cooperation.

4　Words and phrases

sincerely B [sɪnˈsɪəli]/A [sɪnˈsɪrli] *adv.* 真诚地
carry-on baggage 随身携带的行李
window shade 遮光板
tray table 小桌板
taxiing [tækˈsɪŋ] *v.* 滑行

5　Notes to the announcements

(1) We will be sincerely at your service.
我们将竭诚为您服务。
(2) The captain has turned on the Fasten Seat Belt Sign, please fasten your seat belt, open the window shade and make sure your seat back and tray table are in the full upright position.

广播音频

机长已经打开安全带指示灯,请系好您的安全带,打开遮光板,调直座椅靠背,收起小桌板。

Part Four Role Play

In small groups, make up a dialogue based on the following situations

(1) Passengers A is travelling with her one-year-old baby for the first time. Help her with her baggage.

(2) Passenger B is travelling with a valuable guitar. Help him stow his baggage.

Part Five Exercise

1 Translate the following phrases into English

(1) 随身携带的行李　　　　　　(2) 前方座椅的下面
(3) 可折叠的婴儿车　　　　　　(4) 占座座位
(5) 安全要求　　　　　　　　　(6) 遮光板
(7) 机长　　　　　　　　　　　(8) 手提箱
(9) 背包　　　　　　　　　　　(10) 中国国际航空公司
(11) 衣橱隔间　　　　　　　　　(12) 贵重物品

2 Translate the following sentences into English

(1) 需要我帮您放行李吗?
(2) 这样会给您同排的旅客带来不便。
(3) 您头顶上方的行李架已经满了,要不您把行李交给我?
(4) 我来帮您收好婴儿车,放在您头顶上方的行李架上。
(5) 在飞机滑行、起飞、颠簸和降落时,请不要打开您头顶上方的行李架。

3 Translate the following sentences into Chinese

(1) The baggage is usually stored in the overhead compartment or under the seat in front of you.

(2) I'll look after it for you with care.

(3) Since your vase is fragile and valuable, please take good care of it during the flight.

(4) According to the safety instructions, the baggage can't be placed on the aisle or by the emergency exits.

(5) Thank you for your understanding and cooperation.

4 Fill in the blanks in the following dialogues

Dialogue 1

CA: Good morning, Miss. ＿＿＿＿＿(1)＿＿＿＿＿ (请问需要什么帮助吗)?

PAX: Good morning! You know this is my first time traveling by air. _____(2)_____ (我不知道怎么放行李).

CA: Well. _____(3)_____ (行李通常放在头顶上方的行李架或者前方座椅的下面).

PAX: Got it. My roller bag is too heavy. _____(4)_____ (可以帮我一起放到行李架上吗)?

CA: Sure.

Dialogue 2

CA: Excuse me. _____(5)_____ (请问这是哪位旅客的背包)?

PAX: It's mine.

CA: I'm afraid that _____(6)_____ (您不能把它放在过道上). It will block the aisle and bring inconvenience to other people.

PAX: I'm sorry, but I don't know where to place it. _____(7)_____ (我头顶上方的行李架已经满了, 装不了我的背包).

CA: _____(8)_____ (放在您前方座椅的下面可以吗)?

PAX: Actually I want more legroom for my flight.

CA: I see. _____(9)_____ (机舱尾部的行李架还有位置). If you don't mind, I can place your bag there for you.

PAX: Sounds great. Thanks so much.

CA: You are welcome. If _____(10)_____ (需要帮助的话, 请告诉我).

5 Work out the baggage arrangement on board and classify them according to the hint

(1) Be hung on the armrest.

(2) Be placed into the overhead compartment.

(3) Be placed under the seat in front of you.

(4) Be placed by the emergency exits.

(5) Be placed on the aisle.

(6) Be kept by the cabin attendants.

(7) Be hung on the seat back.

(8) Be placed on a vacant seat.

(9) Have an extra seat.

The baggage can:	The baggage can't:

Part Six Supplementary Reading

Baggage Service

If travelling by air, passengers had better have some knowledge about baggage service of airlines.

Baggage can include unchecked baggage and checked baggage. Unchecked baggage can be also called carried-on baggage. Passengers may carry a certain amount of carried-on baggage with them on board. The limits for weight, number of pieces and dimensions of carried-on baggage vary from airline to airline. Carried-on items exceeding limits shall be carried as checked baggage. Passengers will be required to place the baggage in aircraft's cargo compartment.

Airlines often offer free baggage allowance, with which passengers can bring carried-on items or check in a certain amount of baggage for free. If baggage exceeds the allowance, passengers have to pay for the exceeding part.

Airlines have clear rules on what can be carried and what cannot be brought onto the plane. Passengers are not allowed to carry such items as explosive articles, controlled knives, drugs, lighters when travelling by air. Small animals complying with the rules can only be transported as checked baggage which means that they are forbidden to be carried into the cabin. Articles like currency, jewelry, electronic equipment for personal life or entertainment can be carried with the passengers into the cabin. What's more, there are specific requirements for certain items. Regulations on some commonly used items are listed as follows.

Portable lithium batteries between 100 Wh and 160 Wh can be only carried into the aircraft as carried-on baggage and each passenger cannot carry more than two batteries.

Liquid articles like gels and aerosols must be stored in containers with a maximum capacity of 100 mL. Containers for liquids should be placed in a resealable transparent plastic bag with a maximum volume of no more than 1 L. If containers are larger than 100 mL (even if it is not full) and more than one plastic bag are carried, they are not allowed to be carried into the cabin but as checked baggage.

If passengers travel with a baby, only a collapsible stroller which meets the size required by the airline can be carried into the cabin.

For valuable items like fragile crafts or some musical instruments, passengers can buy an extra seat, which means such items can occupy a seat in the cabin and passengers can take better care of the valuables. What needs to be kept in mind is that the package of such items should meet the requirements of airlines.

The baggage may sometimes fail to reach the destinations on time or even get lost. If these situations occur, passengers can turn to the airlines. They will make every effort to locate passengers' baggage, but if failed to find the baggage, a compensation will be paid to the passengers. In addition, if the baggage is damaged on the part of the airlines,

passengers can also ask for compensation within a certain period of time.

All in all, what passengers should keep in mind is that the specific regulations of baggage service vary from airline to airline. In case of unnecessary trouble, passengers had better check the requirements online or by telephone before travelling.

Decide the following statements are true (T) or false (F) according to the passage

(1) Baggage can include unchecked baggage, checked baggage and carried-on baggage. (   )

(2) All baggage carried by the passengers is free on board. (   )

(3) Passengers are forbidden to carry fireworks on board. (   )

(4) A collapsible stroller of any size can be carried into the cabin. (   )

(5) Valuable baggage can occupy a vacant seat for free. (   )

(6) As long as the baggage is damaged, passengers can ask for compensation. (   )

Unit 4　Safety Check

Learning Objectives

1. Be familiar with various dialogues and announcements for safety check service.
2. Grasp relevant English expressions.
3. Know how to check the cabin.
4. Know the cabin attendants' responsibilities.

Part One　Listening

 Listen to the dialogue and choose the best answer to each question

(1) Are the passengers allowed to remove emergency equipment on board?

A. Yes

B. No

(2) What is the passenger removing?

A. Oxygen mask

B. Life jacket

C. Seat belt

听力音频

2 Listen to the dialogue and fill in the blanks

(The purser asks a cabin attendant to check the equipment on board.)

CA: cabin attendant   P: purser

P: Excuse me, Cindy?

CA: What can I do for you, Miss Li?

P: I wonder if you can help me _____(1)_____?

CA: _____(2)_____.

P: Well, I hope you can check the equipment which is at or around your crew station as stated in your _____(3)_____, and make sure all equipment is _____(4)_____ or _____(5)_____.

CA: OK, got it.

Part Two   Dialogues

CA: cabin attendant   PAX: passenger

1 Dialogue 1

(Two cabin attendants are talking about their pre-flight check.)

CA1: Hi, Cindy. What are you doing here?

CA2: I'm checking the galley.

CA1: Have you finished?

CA2: No, I've just finished checking emergency equipment, oven and water heater. Next, I'm going to check the total portions and quality of drinks and food. It can be finished very shortly. How about you?

CA1: I've just arranged the magazines and newspapers in good order. And now I'm going to report to the purser.

CA2: See you then.

CA1: See you.

2 Dialogue 2

(A passenger is going to the lavatory.)

CA: Excuse me, sir. Would you please return to your seat?

PAX: Why? I'm going to the lavatory.

CA: Sorry, sir. The plane is about to take off. You must remain seated with your seat belt fastened. You'll have to wait until the plane reaches its cruising altitude. It won't take long.

PAX: All right.

CA: Thank you for your cooperation.

3 Dialogue 3

(A passenger doesn't know how to fasten the seat belt.)

CA: Excuse me, Miss. Please fasten your seat belt.

PAX: Oh, but I don't know how to do it.

CA: Never mind. Let me help you. Just slip the belt into the buckle and pull tight. Look, just like this. That's all.

PAX: Thank you. By the way, how long will it take to fly from Shanghai to Guangzhou?

CA: Our flying time should be approximately 2 hours and 22 minutes.

PAX: At what altitude?

CA: We will be flying at an altitude of about 8700 meters.

PAX: And what is the speed of our plane?

CA: The cruising speed will be about 900 kilometers per hour.

PAX: Thank you for answering my questions.

PAX: It's my pleasure.

4 Dialogue 4

(A passenger puts his hand luggage in the aisle.)

CA: Excuse me, sir. Could you put your luggage into the overhead compartment? It is blocking the aisle.

PAX: I'm awfully sorry, but I cannot reach there.

CA: I will help you to do so.

PAX: Thank you. You are so kind.

CA: You are welcome.

5 Dialogue 5

(A passenger is using the laptop computer.)

CA: Excuse me, sir. Would you please stop using your laptop computer and put it away?

PAX: Why? I'm working on an important program.

CA: You are not allowed to do so because the plane will take off soon. Using computers during take-off might interfere with the navigation system.

PAX: When can I use it?

CA: You can use it when the plane enters its cruising altitude.

PAX: OK.

CA: Thank you for your cooperation.

6 Words and expressions

emergency B [ɪˈmɜːdʒənsi]/A[ɪˈmɜːrdʒənsi] *n.* 紧急情况；突发事件

equipment [ɪˈkwɪpmənt] *n.* 设备；装备；器材

lavatory B [ˈlævətri]/A [ˈlævətɔːri] *n.* 厕所；盥洗室

approximately B[əˈprɒksɪmətli]/A[əˈprɑːksɪmətli] *adv.* 大约；大概
laptop computer 手提电脑
interfere with 干涉；干扰；妨碍
navigation [ˌnævɪˈgeɪʃn] *n.* 航行；航海；导航
cruise [kruːz] *v. & n.* 巡航；巡游

7 Notes to the dialogues

(1) You must remain seated with your seat belt fastened.
您需要坐好，并系好安全带。
(2) Our flying time should be approximately 2 hours and 22 minutes.
我们的飞行时间大约是 2 小时 22 分钟。
(3) Could you put your luggage into the overhead compartment?
您可以将行李放置到头顶上方的行李架上吗？
(4) Using computers during take-off might interfere with the navigation system.
起飞过程中使用电脑会干扰导航系统。

Part Three　Announcements

广播音频

1 Safety check

Ladies and gentlemen,
　　The airplane is taxiing into the runway for take-off. Flight attendants will start safety checks. Please return your seat back to the upright position, stow your tray table and footrest, open the window shade and check that your seat belt is securely fastened. All electronic devices must be switched off at this time.
　　Thank you for your cooperation.

2 Baggage arrangement

Ladies and gentlemen,
　　May I have your attention, please? Please make sure that your hand baggage is stored in the overhead locker. Small articles can be put under the seat in front of you. Please keep the aisle clear for others to go through.
　　Thank you!

3 Dimming the cabin light

Ladies and Gentlemen,
　　Before take-off, we'll dim the cabin light.
　　If you would like to read, please turn on the reading light, the switch is located on your armrest or on the overhead service panel.
　　Thank you!

4 Words and phrases

check [tʃek] *v.* & *n.* 检查;核对
safety ['seɪfti] *n.* 安全
footrest ['fʊtrest] *n.* 脚踏板
taxi ['tæksi] *v.* (飞机)滑行
upright ['ʌpraɪt] *adj.* 垂直的;直立的
runway ['rʌnweɪ] *n.* 飞机跑道
aisle [aɪl] *n.* 走道;过道
dim [dɪm] *adj.* 暗淡的;昏暗的 *v.* 使变暗
armrest B ['ɑːmrest] / A ['ɑːrmrest] *n.* 扶手;靠手
panel ['pænl] *n.* 仪表板;嵌板

Part Four Role Play

In small groups, make up a dialogue based on the following situations

(1) Cabin crew are preparing for take-off. A passenger is still using the table and the footrest. A cabin attendant comes up to stop him.

(2) The captain has just switched the seat belt sign on. A cabin attendant, Linda, saw a passenger stand on the aisle.

Part Five Exercise

1 Fill in the blanks in the following dialogues

Dialogue 1

CA: Excuse me, sir. Please put out your cigarette immediately. _____(1)_____ (这里禁止吸烟)!

PAX: OK. I'm sorry. By the way, is there any smoking section _____(2)_____ (在客舱里)?

CA: No, there isn't. _____(3)_____ (根据中国民航总局的规定), smoking is forbidden on all flights.

Dialogue 2

CA: Excuse me, sir. I'd like to remind you that passengers are not allowed to remove _____(4)_____ (紧急设备) by themselves. Please put back the _____(5)_____ (救生衣).

PAX: Oh, I'm sorry.

2 Translate the following phrases into English

(1) 电子设备 (2) 应急出口
(3) 座椅扶手 (4) 导航设备
(5) 安全带指示灯 (6) 巡航高度
(7) 客舱乘务员各就各位 (8) 笔记本电脑
(9) 漂浮装置 (10) 前排旅客座椅下方

3 Translate the following sentences into English

(1) 请将您的座椅靠背调到垂直状态。
(2) 所有的电子设备都需要关闭。
(3) 为了您的安全，我请求您回到座位上。
(4) 请您关闭移动电话好吗？
(5) 请确保您的手提行李已放到头顶上方的行李架内。

4 Translate the following sentences into Chinese

(1) We are preparing for take-off.
(2) Could you please return to your seat, sir?
(3) May I ask you to open the window shade?
(4) Please tell the cabin attendant if you need any help.
(5) I'm sorry, sir. Smoking is prohibited.

Part Six Supplementary Reading

Hand luggage Limit

Hand luggage is any type of small luggage that can be carried by hand. These units are fairly small and lightweight, and they are typically designed for carrying fewer objects than larger pieces of luggage. Hand luggage is usually even smaller than carry-on luggage that fits in overhead compartment on airplanes, though some pieces of hand luggage can be somewhat larger. In most cases, these pieces of luggage only feature a handle or shoulder strap, though some may feature telescoping handles and wheels for rolling the unit across airports, train stations, hotel lobbies and so on.

The terms "hand luggage" and "carry-on luggage" are often used interchangeably. When this definition is used, hand luggage can be fairly large, as long as it is not so large as to be unable to fit in an overhead compartment. Carry-on luggage very often features a telescoping handle for easy pulling across airports, and wheels to help the luggage glide smoothly. Sometimes the luggage is stackable; one piece is fairly small and features wheels and the telescoping handle, and another piece can stack on top of the rolling piece and secure to the telescoping handle, thereby making one unit for transport.

Hand luggage may refer to small pieces of luggage that can be carried by hand or stored easily in overhead compartment.

The materials used to make hand luggage can vary. The materials are usually fairly durable to withstand the rigors of travelling, and they may range from natural materials such as cotton or canvas to synthetic materials such as nylon, polyester, or even plastic. Some carry-on luggage features a hard shell to protect fragile items, especially electronics. Hard shell hand luggage is not as easily stored, however, the hard shell will prevent from compacting. Soft shell luggage can often be compacted slightly to fit more easily in overhead compartment or even in trunks of cars.

A broader definition of the term hand luggage may include any small piece of luggage, regardless of design, that can be carried by hand and stored fairly easily in overhead compartment. This means certain duffel bags and purses may fit the definition as well. Hard shell cases can also fit the definition, regardless of whether those cases are intended for use as luggage. Other carry-on items, such as musical instruments, may be considered carry-on luggage, depending on the context, and in many cases, airlines will not charge for storage of such items as long as they fit the size restrictions outlined by the airlines before boarding a plane.

Decide the following statements are true (T) or false (F) according to the passage

(1) Hand luggage is any type of small luggage that can be carried by hand. (   )

(2) Sometimes hand luggage is too large to fit in an overhead compartment. (   )

(3) The terms "hand luggage" and "carry-on luggage" are often used interchangeably. (   )

(4) The materials used to make hand luggage can vary. (   )

(5) Soft shell luggage can often be compacted slightly to fit more easily in overhead compartment or even in trunks of cars. (   )

Module 2 In-flight Service

Unit 5 Beverage and Meal Service

Learning Objectives

1. Be familiar with various dialogues and announcements for beverage and meal service.
2. Grasp relevant English expressions.
3. Know how to give announcements before serving beverages and meals.
4. Know how to serve special meals.

Part One   Listening

1 Listen to the dialogue and choose the best answer to each question

(1) What does the passenger order for beverage?
A. Coke
B. Sprite
C. Fanta

(2) What kind of drinks are there on board?
A. Soft drinks, mineral water, tea
B. Soft drinks, coffee, tea, beer
C. Soft drinks, juice, mineral water, tea, coffee and beer

2 Listen to the dialogue and fill in the blanks

(A cabin attendant is offering beverages.)
CA: cabin attendant   PAX: passenger
CA: Excuse me, sir. Would you _____(1)_____ a drink?
PAX: Yes. What kind of drinks do you have on _____(2)_____?

CA: We have _____(3)_____ as well as tea, coffee and soda.

PAX: I'd like a cup of coffee. Thank you. By the way, when will our meals be _____(4)_____?

CA: We will serve a _____(5)_____ with the beverages first. Lunch will be served a few hours after departure.

PAX: Oh, I see. Thank you very much.

CA: My pleasure. If you need any help, please don't hesitate to contact our cabin attendants.

Part Two Dialogues

CA: cabin attendant   PAX: passenger

1 Dialogue 1

(A cabin attendant is serving liquor.)

CA: Excuse me, madam. Would you like something to drink before dinner?

PAX: I'd like a gin and tonic, please.

CA: I'm sorry, madam. I'm afraid we don't have gin and tonic on board. Would you like something else? We have Cinzano and Scotch.

PAX: All right. I'll have a Cinzano.

CA: How would you like your Cinzano, madam?

PAX: On the rocks.

CA: Certainly, madam. Please wait a moment.

2 Dialogue 2

(A cabin attendant is serving beverage.)

PAX: Excuse me, sir. Today we have soft drinks, juice, mineral water as well as tea and coffee.

CA: What kind of coffee do you have?

PAX: We have Nestle Gold and cappuccino.

CA: How about tea?

PAX: We have jasmine tea and oolong tea.

CA: Jasmine tea, please.

PAX: OK. Here is your tea. It's hot. Be careful.

CA: Thank you.

PAX: You are welcome.

3 Dialogue 3

(First choice unavailable.)

CA: Excuse me, sir. What would you like for dinner? You have a choice of roast beef,

对话音频

steak, chicken and fish.

PAX: I am a vegetarian and I need a vegetarian meal.

CA: Have you ordered a vegetarian meal?

PAX: No. I don't know how to re-book vegetarian meals.

CA: Well, vegetarian meals belongs to special meals. They should be ordered at least 24 hours before the plane takes off, or it will not be available. However, I might be able to find extra servings of vegetables.

PAX: Thank you for your service.

CA: It's my pleasure. If you need any help, you can press the call button over your head.

4 Dialogue 4

(Special meals.)

CA: Excuse me, madam. Have you reserved a baby meal?

PAX: Yes.

CA: I will bring it for you after we start the meal service. If you change your seat, please let me know.

PAX: OK.

CA: Madam, this is the baby meal you ordered.

PAX: Thank you.

5 Dialogue 5

(End of the meal serving of the First Class.)

CA: Excuse me, sir. Would you like more of anything?

PAX: No, thank you. That was enough for me.

CA: How do you like the steak?

PAX: Well, it's great.

CA: May I clear out your table now?

PAX: Sure, go ahead.

6 Words and expressions

gin and tonic 金汤力

cinzano [tʃinˈzɑ: nəu] n. 沁扎诺酒（一种意大利苦艾酒，常用于制作鸡尾酒）

Scotch [skɒtʃ] n. 苏格兰威士忌

on the rocks 加冰

beverage [ˈbevərɪdʒ] n. 饮料

soft drink 软饮料（不含酒精）

mineral water 矿泉水

Nestle Gold 雀巢金牌（咖啡）

cappuccino B[kæpuˈtʃi: nəu]/A[kæpuˈti: nou] n. 卡布奇诺

oolong tea 乌龙茶
jasmine tea 茉莉花茶
unavailable [ˌʌnəˈveɪləbl] adj. 难以获得的
roast beef 烤牛肉
steak [steɪk] n. 牛排
vegetarian B[ˌvedʒəˈteərɪən]/A[ˌvedʒəˈterərɪən] n. 素食主义者
rebook 重新订票
reserve B[rɪˈzɜːv]/A[rɪˈzɜːrv] v. 预订（座位等）
clear out 清除

7 Notes to the dialogues

(1) I'm afraid we don't have gin and tonic on board.
抱歉，本次航班上没有金汤力。

(2) You have a choice of roast beef, steak, chicken and fish.
本次航班的主食有烤牛肉、牛排、鸡肉和鱼肉。

(3) If you need any help, you can press the call button over your head.
如果您需要任何帮助，您可以按您头顶上方的呼唤铃。

(4) Have you reserved a baby meal?
您提前预订了婴儿餐吗？

Part Three Announcements

1 Announcement before the meal service

Ladies and gentlemen,

We are pleased to begin our meal service. Flight attendants will be moving through the cabin serving meals and beverages soon.

Please put down your tray table in front of you. For the convenience of the passengers behind you, please return your seat back to the upright position during the meal service. If you have any special diet requirements, please feel free to contact any of our cabin attendants.

Thank you!

广播音频

2 Announcement for unavailable service

Ladies and gentlemen,

We are sorry to inform you that hot drinks are not available on this flight because the water system is out of order. However, we can serve you cold drinks. We apologize for the inconvenience caused. Your understanding will be greatly appreciated.

3 Announcement of the meal service

Ladies and gentlemen,

We will be serving you lunch with tea, coffee and other soft drinks soon. We are offering you choices of chicken, beef and fish. If you have any special diet requirements, please tell the cabin attendants.

For your convenience, please put down the tray table and put your seat back upright for the comfort of the passengers behind you.

Hope you enjoy our in-flight meal service. Thank you.

4 Announcement of the refreshment service

Ladies and gentlemen,

Now we are going to serve you refreshment. We will be offering you tea, coffee, fruit juice, coke, Sprite and mineral water. You are welcome to make your choice. Please put down your tray table and adjust your seat back to the upright position for the comfort of the passengers behind you.

Hope you enjoy our in-flight meal service. Thank you.

5 Words and phrases

out of order 发生故障
convenience [kənˈviːniəns] *n.* 便利；方便
appreciate [əˈpriːʃieɪt] *v.* 欣赏；感激
comfort B[ˈkʌmfət]/A[ˈkʌmfərt] *n.* 安慰；舒适
Sprite [spraɪt] 雪碧

Part Four   Role Play

In small groups, make up a dialogue based on the following situations

(1) Passenger A is asking for more fish, but there isn't any left. A cabin attendant is recommending other food.

(2) Passenger B is hungry and asks for something to eat and you offer him several kinds of meals on board to choose.

Part Five   Exercise

1 Fill in the blanks in the following dialogues

Dialogue 1

CA: Excuse me, sir. We will be serving lunch soon. _____(1)_____ (午餐前您想喝

点什么呢)?

PAX: _____(2)_____(我想喝一杯威士忌).

CA: _____(3)_____(不好意思,本次航班上没有威士忌。给您来一杯葡萄酒可以吗)?

PAX: All right. I'll have a glass of wine. _____(4)_____(顺便问一下,午餐主菜有什么)?

CA: _____(5)_____(午餐主菜有牛肉、鸡肉和鱼肉).

PAX: It sounds great. Thank you.

CA: My pleasure.

Dialogue 2

PAX: _____(6)_____(您好,我能点一些喝的吗)?

CA: Yes, _____(7)_____(我们为您准备了果汁、咖啡、茶和苏打水,您想喝点什么呢)?

CA: _____(8)_____(给我来一杯橙汁).

PAX: OK, please wait a moment. Here you are.

CA: _____(9)_____(请问什么时候供应晚餐)?

PAX: _____(10)_____(我们先为您提供饮料和小吃。晚餐将会在1小时内供应).

PAX: Oh, I see. Thanks so much.

CA: You are welcome. If _____(11)_____(需要帮助的话,请按呼叫按钮).

2 Translate the following phrases into English

(1) 乌龙茶　　　　　　　　(2) 加冰

(3) 果汁　　　　　　　　　(4) 矿泉水

(5) 特殊餐食要求　　　　　(6) 菊花茶

(7) 婴儿餐　　　　　　　　(8) 素食

(9) 小吃　　　　　　　　　(10) 苏打水

3 Translate the following sentences into English

(1) 我们将马上为您提供晚餐,主菜种类有鸡肉、牛肉和鱼肉。

(2) 请问您想喝点什么?

(3) 今天我们为您准备了果汁、矿泉水、软饮、咖啡和茶。

(4) 为方便您后排的旅客用餐,请您调直座椅靠背。

(5) 如您有特殊餐食要求,请联系我们的乘务员。

4 Translate the following sentences into Chinese

(1) We are sorry to inform you that hot drinks are not available on this flight because the water system is out of order.

(2) Please put down your tray table in front of you.

(3) I'm afraid we don't have gin and tonic on board.

(4) We apologize for the inconvenience caused.

(5) We are offering you choices of chicken, beef and fish.

Part Six　Supplementary Reading

In-flight Meal Service

In-flight meal service is one of the main aspects of cabin service. All airlines make every effort to provide satisfactory food and beverages for passengers. To provide good in-flight meal service for the passengers requires a lot of training and planning and attention to details. According to flying time, routes and classes, the food is different.

For first and business class, the service should be more elaborate so that passengers may have a feeling that they are feasting in a fine restaurant with many choices of meals and beverages. Passengers with different tastes can have their preferred choices. To meet passengers' different needs of drinks, all the airlines will prepare wine, tea, coffee, juice, water' etc.

For economy class, passengers' choices are quite limited. Generally, the food is portioned out and served directly to the passengers from the trolley. The service procedures are much simpler than those in the first and business class. In order to offer satisfactory service to the passengers, many airlines have taken the different dietary backgrounds into consideration. For example, Asian people prefer rice while Westerners prefer potatoes, some people like beef and chicken while others prefer seafood.

For those passengers who have special diet requirements, special meal orders should be made at least 24 hours before the departure, otherwise it will not be available. If passengers want to change the pre-booked meals, they should do it more than 24 hours prior to the flight departure time. If the price of the new meal booked is higher than the original meal, passengers should be responsible for the price difference.

Decide whether the following statements are true (T) or false (F) according to the passage

(1) Special meals should be ordered no more than 24 hours before the plane takes off. (　　)

(2) The airlines should pay for the price difference when the passengers change their pre-booked meals before the flight departure time. (　　)

(3) The meal service in first and business class section is more complex than that in economy class section. (　　)

(4) In-flight meal service is not so important for the cabin attendants. (　　)

(5) For economy class, passengers' choices of meals are not limited. (　　)

Unit 6　In-flight Entertainment Service

Learning Objectives

1. Be familiar with various in-flight entertainment announcements.
2. Grasp relevant English expressions.
3. Know how to provide in-flight entertainment service.
4. Know how to operate the in-flight entertainment devices.

Part One　Listening

1 Listen to the dialogue and choose the best answer to each question

(1) What can the passengers do if they feel bored during the flight?
A. They can read magazines and newspapers.
B. Nothing.
C. They can read books.

(2) How long will this flight take?
A. Two hours
B. One hour
C. Three hours

2 Listen to the dialogue and fill in the blanks

(A cabin attendant is telling the passenger how to use the entertainment device.)

CA: cabin attendant　PAX: passenger

PAX: Excuse me, madam. Can you do me a _____(1)_____?

CA: Of course. What can I do for you?

PAX: My son wants to watch cartoons, but I don't know how to _____(2)_____ the device?

CA: Let me help you. First, press the _____(3)_____ on your armrest. Then _____(4)_____ the channel corresponding to the cartoons. After that, you can enjoy it.

PAX: Thank you very much.

CA: You are welcome. Hope you will have a good time on board.

听力音频

Part Two   Dialogues

CA: cabin attendant   PAX: passenger

1 Dialogue 1

(A passenger is asking for another headset.)

PAX: Excuse me, madam. I was wondering if I could have another headset.

CA: Of course. But why?

PAX: The headset in the seat pocket doesn't work.

CA: OK. Let me have a check... Well, it's broken. Please wait a moment. I'll get you another one. Here you are.

PAX: Thank you very much. By the way, I don't like this program. I'd like to watch movies. Can you help me adjust it?

CA: Certainly. The movies we have on board include comedy, action and feature movies. Which would you like to watch?

PAX: I prefer comedy. Which channel is it?

CA: The first channel. Have you got it?

PAX: Yes. Thank you for your help.

CA: My pleasure.

2 Dialogue 2

(A passenger feels bored.)

PAX: Excuse me, sir. When will we arrive at Beijing Capital International airport?

CA: At 10:30.

PAX: That means we have to stay on the plane for 4 hours. It's too long. I will feel bored if I have nothing to do.

CA: To enrich your experience on board, we have prepared movies, selected TV features, music, games and route maps for you.

PAX: Do you have newspapers?

CA: Yes. We have *Xinjing Newspaper*, *Economics Daily*, *Global Times* and *Beijing Youth*. Which one do you want?

PAX: *Economics Daily*, please.

CA: May I turn on the reading light for you?

PAX: Yes. Thank you for your kind help.

CA: You are welcome. Wish you a pleasant trip.

3 Dialogue 3

(A passenger can't find the headsets.)

PAX: Excuse me, sir. Can you help me?

CA：Of course. What can I do for you?

PAX：I want to listen to music, but I can't find the headset.

CA：The headsets are in the seat pocket in front of you. Have you seen it?

PAX：Yes. But I have problems with the control unit.

CA：Let me show you. Just press this button to select the channel corresponding to the music you want to listen to.

PAX：OK, I got it. Do you have any recommendations about the music?

CA：Folk music, classic music, pop music and Chinese Opera are available on this flight. What kind of music do you like?

PAX：Folk music, please.

CA：OK, just enjoy it.

4 Dialogue 4

(A passenger asks for the tourist brochures.)

CA：Excuse me, madam. May I turn on the reading light for you?

PAX：Yes. Thank you for your kind help. By the way, do you have tourist brochures?
　　　I'm going to have a holiday in Italy, and I'd like to go around Rome.

CA：Yes, we have. An English one or a Chinese one?

PAX：A Chinese one, please.

CA：OK, I'll get it for you right away.

PAX：Thank you.

5 Words and expressions

program B['prəʊgræm]/A['proʊgræm] *n.* 程序；计划；节目

comedy B['kɒmədi]/A['kɑːmədi] *n.* 喜剧

action movie 动作片

feature ['fiːtʃə(r)] *n.* 特色；特征；特写或专题节目

channel ['tʃænl] *n.* 电视台；频道

Xinjing Newspaper 新京报

Economics Daily 经济日报

Global Times 环球时报

Beijing Youth 北京青年报

corresponding with 与……符合；与……一致

recommendation [rekəmen'deɪʃn] *n.* 推荐

folk music 民俗音乐

classic music 古典音乐

pop music 流行音乐

brochure B['brəʊʃə(r)]/A[broʊ'ʃʊr] *n.* 手册

6 Notes to the dialogues

(1) The movies we have on board include comedy, action and feature movies.

今天我们为您准备的影片有喜剧片、动作片、剧情片。

(2) To enrich your experience on board, we have prepared movies, selected TV features, music, games and route maps for you.

为了丰富您的旅途生活,我们为您准备了电影、精编电视短片、音乐、游戏及航线图。

(3) Do you have any recommendations about the music?

有什么好的音乐推荐吗?

(4) May I turn on the reading light for you?

我帮您打开阅读灯好吗?

Part Three Announcements

1 Introduction to in-flight entertainment system

Ladies and gentlemen,

To enrich your experience on board, we will turn on the personal entertainment system. We have prepared movies, music, games and other programs. For more details, please refer to the In-flight Entertainment Guide in the seat pocket in front of you. Thank you!

2 Introduction to programs on board

Ladies and gentlemen,

We will be showing you a movie. Please use the headsets in the seat pocket in front of you. You can choose channel 1 or 2 to select the language you like. If you have any problems, please feel free to contact our flight attendants. We hope you enjoy the movie.

3 Collect headsets

Ladies and gentlemen,

We will arrive at Beijing Capital International Airport soon. The in-flight entertainment will be switched off for landing. The cabin attendants will be walking through the cabin to collect the headsets from you. Please get your headsets ready. Thank you.

4 Local area Wi-Fi networks

Ladies and gentlemen,

Our in-flight Local Area Networks is now available. Activate the Wi-Fi function on your laptop, and you can access various online information and services. The operation guide is in the seat pocket in front of you. For your safety, please ensure that your mobile phones remain switched off during the flight. Thank you.

5 Words and phrases

In-flight Entertainment Guide 机上娱乐系统指南
switch [swɪtʃ] *n.* 开关 *v.* 转换；替换；调换
activate [ˈæktɪveɪt] *v.* 刺激；激活
function [ˈfʌŋkʃn] *n.* 功能；职责
access [ˈækses] *n.* 通道；进入；使用权

Part Four   Role Play

In small groups, make up a dialogue based on the following situations

(1) Passenger A doesn't know how to select the movie channel.

(2) Passenger B feels bored of the long-distance flight, so you recommend him to read some duty-free brochures.

Part Five   Exercise

1 Fill in the blanks in the following dialogue

CA：Excuse me, sir. ＿＿＿＿＿＿(1)＿＿＿＿＿＿（请问您是否需要一份报纸）？

PAX：＿＿＿＿＿(2)＿＿＿＿＿（有《环球时报》吗）？

CA：＿＿＿＿＿(3)＿＿＿＿＿（不好意思，本次航班没有《环球时报》，请问《经济日报》可以吗）？

PAX：All right. ＿＿＿＿＿(4)＿＿＿＿＿（我还有一个问题，我的女儿想要听音乐，请问如何使用这个娱乐设备）？

CA：＿＿＿＿＿(5)＿＿＿＿＿（您可以按这个按钮选择您想要看的节目）。

PAX：OK, I got it. Thank you for your help.

CA：My pleasure.

2 Translate the following phrases into English

(1) 机上娱乐指南   (2) 无线局域网
(3) 阅读灯   (4) 动作片
(5) 频道   (6) 耳机
(7) 宣传册   (8) 切断(电源)
(9) 民俗音乐   (10) 流行音乐

3 Translate the following sentences into English

(1) 机上娱乐系统操作指南在您前方座椅口袋里面。

(2) 为了丰富您的旅途生活，我们为您准备了电影、音乐、游戏等。

(3) 乘务员将在客舱内走动收回耳机。

(4) 请激活无线网络功能。

(5) 请问有旅游宣传册吗？

4 Translate the following sentences into Chinese

(1) We have *Xinjing Newspaper*, *Economics Daily*, *Global Times* and *Beijing Youth*.

(2) We hope you enjoy the movie.

(3) Our in-flight Local Area Networks is now available.

(4) For your safety, please ensure that your mobile phones remain switched off during the flight.

(5) Please use the headsets in the seat pocket in front of you.

Part Six Supplementary Reading

In-flight Entertainment Equipment

In-flight entertainment refers to the system that an airline provides entertainment to its passengers during a long time. Passengers can watch movies, listen to music or read newspapers to kill the time during the flight.

Usually on the flights of Chinese airlines, flight attendants will prepare newspapers both in Chinese and English. There are also magazines, tourist brochures and duty-free brochures in the seat pocket in front of the passengers. Every passenger can find the reading materials he or she is interested in on the flight. In addition, passengers can enjoy both Western and Chinese music, such as pop music, classical music, country music and so on.

Take China Southern Airlines for example, there is a passenger control unit (PCU) on the armrest of the narrow-body aircraft. Passengers can change the channel and volume with it. The reading light button and the call button are also on the PCU. Every passenger can enjoy the movie played on the overhead TV or listen to the music he or she has selected. On the wide-body aircraft, advanced TV sets are available. Passengers can enjoy plenty of movies, TV programs and audio programs. The touch screen makes them very easy to operate. They can even play games on the TV sets. The TV sets also provide E-books so that passengers can read books.

All the airlines would like to make every flight comfortable and enjoyable for its passengers.

Decide whether the following statements are true (T) or false (F) according to the passage

(1) Passengers can enjoy movies, play games and listen to music on board. (   )

(2) PCU stands for personal control unit. (   )

(3) The reading light button and the call button are also on the PCU on the narrow-body aircraft. (   )

(4) Only Chinese newspapers are provided on the flights. (   )

(5) In-flight entertainment refers to the system that an airline provides entertainment to its passengers during a long time. (   )

Unit 7 Medical Service

Learning Objectives

1. Be familiar with various dialogues and announcements for medical service.
2. Grasp relevant English expressions.
3. Know how to offer medical service.
4. Know the cabin attendants' responsibilities.

Part One Listening

1 Listen to the dialogue and choose the best answer to each question

(1) What's wrong with the passenger?
A. She is ill.
B. Her ankle is sprained.
C. She has a stomachache.

(2) What does the cabin attendant take for the passenger?
A. Hot water
B. Medicine
C. Cold compress

2 Listen to the dialogue and fill in the blanks

(A passenger has just sprained her ankle.)
CA: What's wrong with your foot? Can I help you?
M: Thank you. I sprained my _____(1)_____ just now. It _____(2)_____.
CA: I'm sorry to hear that, madam. _____(3)_____. I can see the joint here is swelling up.
M: Thank you for your patience. _____(4)_____.

CA: Don't worry. I will get _____(5)_____ for you.

M: Thank you.

Part Two Dialogues

CA: cabin attendant   PAX: passenger

1 Dialogue 1

对话音频

(A passenger is suffering from airsickness.)

CA: You look rather pale. Can I help you?

PAX: Yes, please. I am feeling sick and dizzy. I feel like throwing up.

CA: You are suffering from airsickness. Here is an airsickness bag.

PAX: Can you help me go to the toilet?

CA: Sorry, sir, but I think it's not safe alone there for you. Here is an airsickness bag. And you can lie down and have a rest. Here is a cup of water to rinse out your mouth if you vomit.

PAX: Thank you.

CA: Not at all. If your airsickness is getting worse, please call us immediately. If you need some medicine for airsickness, I'll get it for you right away.

PAX: OK!

2 Dialogue 2

(A passenger presses the call button.)

CA: Did you press the call button? What's the matter?

PAX: Yes. I'm afraid I have caught a cold. I have a sore throat and my nose is stuffed up.

CA: I'm sorry to hear that, madam. What can I do for you?

PAX: Could you give me something hot to drink?

CA: Certainly, madam. What would you like to drink?

PAX: Can you give me some hot water?

CA: Of course. And towels using for hot compresses may relieve the discomfort of a stuffy nose.

PAX: Thanks so much.

CA: It's my pleasure. I will be back in a minute.

3 Dialogue 3

(A passenger is suffering from indigestion.)

CA: What can I do for you, sir?

PAX: Oh, I have a pain in my stomach.

CA: What kind of pain, sir?

PAX: A pain in the middle of my stomach.

CA: Have you had this pain before?

PAX: No, I don't think so.

CA: Is there any pain elsewhere, sir? I mean the pain in your arms, or in your back.

PAX: No, no ... Just here in the middle.

CA: Are your fingers tingling?

PAX: Not really.

CA: Have you eaten something in a hurry?

PAX: Hmm ... Yes. I just had some spicy food before boarding the plane.

CA: I think you are suffering from indigestion. Shall I bring you some medicine?

PAX: Yes, thank you.

4 Dialogue 4

CA: Did you press the call button, madam? What can I do for you?

PAX: Yes, Miss. My eardrums hurt and the booming sound of the plane seems to fade away, just like something blocking my ears.

CA: Don't worry, madam. Most passengers have this kind of feeling. It is caused by the change of air pressure. That is because of the decompression.

PAX: What can I do to relieve it?

CA: You can relieve the earache simply by swallowing or sucking sweets.

PAX: I will have a try ... Yes, it works. Thank you.

CA: Not at all.

5 Dialogue 5

(A passenger's nose is bleeding.)

CA: Did you press the call button? What can I do for you?

PAX: Can I get some napkins? My nose is bleeding.

CA: Sir, please bend your head a little bit forward and pinch your nose with your thumb and your finger like this for at least ten minutes. My colleague will get the ice to put on your nose bridge.

PAX: Thank you very much.

CA: It's my responsibility to look after you. Please do not raise your head, otherwise, the blood will run into your throat. It's dangerous. If the bleeding continues after ten minutes, please do another ten minutes.

PAX: I'll have a try ... Yes, it works. Thank you.

CA: It's my pleasure.

6 Words and expressions

airsickness B['eəsɪknəs]/A['eɪˌsɪknɪs] *n.* 晕机

airsickness bag 晕机袋

pale [peɪl] *adj.* 苍白的；无力的
dizzy ['dɪzi] *adj.* 眩晕的
sore throat 喉咙疼痛
hot compress 热敷布；热敷法
earache B['ɪəreɪk]/A ['ɪreɪk] *n.* 耳朵痛；耳痛
fade [feɪd] *v.* 褪色；逐渐消失
nosebleed B['nəʊzbli:d]/A ['noʊzbli:d] *n.* 鼻出血
indigestion [ˌɪndɪ'dʒestʃən] *n.* 消化不良
nose bridge 鼻梁
bleed [bli:d] *v.* 失血；流血

7 Notes to the dialogues

(1) You are suffering from airsickness. Here is an airsickness bag.
您晕机了。这是晕机袋。

(2) You'd better lie down and have a rest.
您最好躺下，休息会。

(3) Did you press the call button? What can I do for you?
您按了呼叫铃吗？我能为您做点什么？

(4) Shall I bring you some medicine?
需要我帮您拿点药过来吗？

Part Three   Announcements

1 A sick passenger on board

广播音频

Ladies and gentlemen,
Your attention please. We need the assistance of a doctor or nurse. If there are any medical professionals on board, please approach one of the cabin attendants immediately. Thank you!

2 Words and phrases

assistance [ə'sɪstəns] *n.* 援助；帮助
nurse B [nɜ:s]/A [nɜ:rs] *n.* 护士；保姆
professional [prə'feʃnl] *adj.* 专业的；职业的 *n.* 专业人员
immediately [ɪ'mi:diətli] *adv.* 立即；即刻

Part Four   Role Play

In small groups, make up a dialogue based on the following situations

(1) Passengers A catches a cold. Offer him some medical service.

(2) Passenger B feels terrible. She needs some hot water.

Part Five Exercise

1 Fill in the blanks in the following dialogue

(A passenger presses the call button.)

CA: Did you press the ＿＿＿＿(1)＿＿＿＿（呼叫铃）? What's the matter?

PAX: Yes. I'm afraid I have caught a cold. I feel cold.

CA: I'm sorry to hear that, madam. Let me take your ＿＿＿＿(2)＿＿＿＿（体温）.

PAX: Thank you.

CA: It's 37.7 ℃. Do you have any other symptoms?

PAX: No. I think it's because I'm in a hurry to catch the plane. I sweat a lot. And it's cold today.

CA: Don't worry, madam. I will get you some hot water and a ＿＿＿＿(3)＿＿＿＿（毯子） to ＿＿＿＿(4)＿＿＿＿（休息一下）. If you have any discomfort, please feel free to tell me. ＿＿＿＿(5)＿＿＿＿（如果有必要的话）, I'll get you some medicine.

PAX: Thanks so much!

CA: It's my pleasure. I will be back in a minute.

2 Translate the following phrases into English

(1) 晕机袋　　　　　　　(2) 喉咙痛

(3) 不适　　　　　　　　(4) 鼻梁

(5) 掌击后背　　　　　　(6) 肩胛

(7) 冷敷布　　　　　　　(8) 受伤的区域

(9) 药物　　　　　　　　(10) 症状

3 Translate the following sentences into English

(1) 您看起来脸色格外苍白。

(2) 对这种情况的处理，我们训练有素。

(3) 听到这个消息我深感遗憾。

(4) 需要我帮您拿点药过来吗?

(5) 您现在感觉如何?

4 Translate the following sentences into Chinese

(1) Let me take your temperature.

(2) I will be back in a minute.

(3) What's the matter?

(4) Let me look at your wounds.

(5) I'm afraid I have caught a cold.

Part Six　Supplementary Reading

High Blood Pressure

What is high blood pressure?

First, let's define high blood pressure. High blood pressure (HBP or hypertension) is when your blood pressure, the force of your blood pushing against the walls of your blood vessels, is consistently too high. High blood pressure increases the risk of heart disease and stroke. High blood pressure is also very common.

High blood pressure usually has no symptoms, so the only way to know if you have it is to get your blood pressure measured. Talk with your doctor about how you can manage your blood pressure and lower your risk.

Prevent High Blood Pressure

Whatever your age is, you can take steps each day to keep your blood pressure in a healthy range. You can help prevent high blood pressure—also called hypertension—by making healthy choices and managing other health conditions you may have.

Practice healthy living habits to help keep your blood pressure in a healthy range. Prevent high blood pressure to help lower your risk for heart disease and stroke.

Manage High Blood Pressure

Lower your risk for problems from high blood pressure, such as heart disease and stroke, by taking steps such as preventing and treating other medical conditions.

Measure your blood pressure on a regular basis. Measuring your blood pressure is an important step toward keeping a healthy blood pressure. Because high blood pressure and elevated blood pressure often have no symptoms, checking your blood pressure is the only way to know for sure whether it is too high.

You can measure your blood pressure at home with a home blood pressure monitor, or you can visit your doctor or nurse to have your blood pressure checked.

If you learn that you have high blood pressure, you should take steps to control your blood pressure to lower your risk of heart disease and stroke.

Blood Pressure Medicines

Many people need to take medicine in addition to making lifestyle changes to help keep their blood pressure at healthy levels.

How do blood pressure medicines work? Blood pressure medicines can work in several different ways. Blood pressure medicines can keep blood pressure at a healthy level by:

• Causing your body to get rid of water, which decreases the amount of water and salt in your body to a healthy level;

• Relaxing your blood vessels;

• Making your heart beat with less force;

• Blocking nerve activity that can restrict your blood vessels.

What are the benefits and risks of blood pressure medicines?

The benefits of blood pressure medicines are clear: Blood pressure medicines can help you keep your blood pressure at healthy levels and therefore greatly reduce the risk of heart disease, heart attack and stroke.

In general, the risks of taking blood pressure medicines are low. However, all medicines have risks. Talk with your doctor or health care professional about the risks of high blood pressure medicines.

Do not stop taking your current medicine without talking to your doctor or health care professional first.

Decide whether the following statements are true (T) or false (F) according to the passage

(1) High blood pressure usually has no symptoms. (   )

(2) You can only visit your doctor or nurse to have your blood pressure checked. (   )

(3) Blood pressure medicines can help you keep your blood pressure at healthy levels. (   )

(4) It is not necessary for us to measure our blood pressure on a regular basis. (   )

(5) The risks of taking blood pressure medicines are low. (   )

Unit 8   Duty-free Service

Learning Objectives

1. Be familiar with various dialogues and announcements for duty-free service.
2. Grasp relevant English expressions.
3. Know how to sell duty-free goods.
4. Know the cabin attendants' responsibilities.

Part One   Listening

1 Listen to the dialogue and choose the best answer to each question

(1) What does the passenger want to buy?

A. Scarf

B. Cigarette

C. Perfume

(2) How much should the passenger pay?

A. 75 US dollars

B. 80 US dollars

C. 120 US dollars

2 Listen to the dialogue and fill in the blanks

(A passenger is inquiring about the duty-free sale on board.)

CA：Would you like to buy some duty-free goods? We have a wide selection on board today.

M：Yes. I'd like five cartons of _____(1)_____.

CA：I'm sorry, sir. As far as I know, visitors to _____(2)_____ are allowed to take _____(3)_____ cigarettes at most.

M：I didn't know about that. All right, two _____(4)_____ of cigarettes, please. How much are they?

CA：That's 75 US dollars, please.

M：Here is 80 US dollars.

CA：Thank you. Here are your _____(5)_____ and your cigarettes. Enjoy your flight.

M：Thank you.

Part Two   Dialogues

CA：cabin attendant   PAX：passenger

1 Dialogue 1

(A passengers is inquiring the duty-free sale on board.)

PAX：Excuse me, Miss. Do you sell duty-free goods on board?

CA：Yes, we provide duty-free sales after the meal service.

PAX：Do you have any spirits I can buy?

CA：Certainly, sir. The duty-free goods magazine in the seat pocket shows our selection.

PAX：Thank you. Could you tell me how many bottles of alcohol I can take to Hong Kong?

CA：One litre of wine is allowed for non-residents and one litre of wine or spirits for residents.

PAX：Thank you!

对话音频

2 Dialogue 2

(A passengers is inquiring about the duty-free sale on board.)

CA: Excuse me, sir. Would you like to buy any duty-free items?

M: Yes, can you tell me something about your duty-free goods?

CA: Of course. We have cigarettes, chocolates, spirits, cosmetics, electronic goods, perfume, skincare products, jewellery, watches and so on.

M: Do you have Chivas Regal?

CA: Certainly, sir. We have it. That'll be 44 US dollars.

M: Do you take RMB?

CA: Yes, sir. We accept US dollars, Euros and RMB.

M: How much is it?

CA: That will be 300 yuan.

M: Here you are.

CA: Thank you.

3 Dialogue 3

(A passenger asks the cabin attendant to recommend the perfume.)

PAX: Excuse me, Miss. I really like the perfume you are wearing.

CA: Thank you for your compliment. This is LV perfume. It's a new perfume and I have been wearing it recently. A lot of people say that it has a very pleasant scent.

PAX: I think so. Where can I buy it?

CA: This perfume is available in our Duty-free Section. You can get the information in your in-flight magazine.

PAX: Thank you. Let me have a look.

PAX: OK, I'll take the 50mL one please. How much is it?

CA: That will be 33 euros. Cash or credit card, madam?

PAX: Um, I only have US dollars. Is that OK?

CA: Certainly, madam. I'll just work out the exchange rate for you. That will be 74 US dollars.

PAX: Here you are.

CA: Thank you very much again for your compliment. Please enjoy your flight.

4 Dialogue 4

CA: Excuse me, sir. Would you like to buy any duty-free items? We have cigarettes, liquor, perfume and pearls.

PAX: Give me a bottle of vodka.

CA: OK, sir. Would you like something else?

PAX: No. That's all. What do I owe you?

CA: It is 19 US dollars, sir.

PAX: Can you give me a discount?

CA: I'm afraid the duty-free items may only be discounted during promotion.

PAX: Here is a traveler's cheque for 50 US dollars.

CA: Would you sign it, please? Thank you, sir. Nineteen dollars out of fifty. Here is your change, sir. Thank you very much.

5 Dialogue 5

(A passenger asks the cabin attendant to recommend a gift for his wife.)

PAX: Miss! Could you come here, please?

CA: May I help you, sir?

PAX: Could you recommend something as a gift for my wife?

CA: OK. How do you like these scarves?

PAX: Oh, it's nice and very Chinese. Is it pure silk?

CA: Yes. Guaranteed pure silk.

PAX: How much is it?

CA: Only 11 US dollars.

PAX: Plus duty?

CA: All the items sold on board are duty-free.

PAX: I'll take it.

6 Words and expressions

spirit ['spɪrɪt] n. 精神；心灵；烈酒
credit card 信用卡
visa ['viːzə] n. 签证
traveler's check 旅行支票
duty-free goods 免税商品
magazine n. 杂志
regulation [ˌreɡjuˈleɪʃn] n. 章程；规则；法规
perfume B ['pɜːfjuːm]/ A [pərˈfjuːm] n. 香水；香味
carton B ['kɑːtn]/A ['kɑːrtn] n. 纸板箱
discount ['dɪskɒunt] n. 折扣

7 Notes to the dialogues

(1) Yes, we provide duty-free sales after the meal service.
是的，我们在餐食服务后会提供免税商品销售服务。

(2) Could you tell me how many bottles of alcohol I can take to Hong Kong?
你能告诉我，去香港能携带几瓶酒吗？

(3) I'm afraid the duty-free items may only be discounted during promotion.
恐怕免税商品只有在促销的时候才打折。

(4) We have cigarettes, liquor, perfume and pearls.
我们有香烟、酒、香水和珍珠。

Part Three　Announcements

1　Duty-free sales

Ladies and gentlemen,

Good morning! Our duty-free shop will open soon. Jewellery, watches, toys, liquor, perfume and cosmetics are all available to purchase on board. Most major currencies, traveler's checks and credit cards are acceptable. For further information, please refer to the sales magazine in your seat pocket.

Thank you!

2　Conclude the duty-free sales

Ladies and gentlemen,

Due to time restriction, we have to conclude the duty-free sales in 15 minutes. Please let us know if you are interested in any duty-free items.

Thank you!

3　Pick up duty-free merchandise

Ladies and gentlemen,

Please pick up your duty-free merchandise at the boarding gate.

Thank you!

4　Words and phrases

jewellery [ˈdʒuːəlri] *n.* 珠宝

liquor [ˈlɪkə(r)] *n.* 烈酒

cosmetic B [kɒzˈmetɪk]/A [kɑːzˈmetɪk] *adj.* 美容的;化妆用的 *n.* 化妆品

purchase B [ˈpɜːtʃəs]/A [ˈpɜːrtʃəs] *v.* 购买;采购

currency B [ˈkʌrənsi]/A [ˈkɜːrənsi] *n.* 货币;通货

restriction [rɪˈstrɪkʃn] *n.* 限制;约束

conclude [kənˈkluːd] *n.* 决定;下结论

merchandise B [ˈmɜːtʃəndaɪs,ˈmɜːtʃəndaɪz]/A [ˈmɜːrtʃəndaɪs,ˈmɜːrtʃəndaɪz] *n.* 商品;货物

boarding gate 登机门

广播音频

Part Four　Role Play

In small groups, make up a dialogue based on the following situations

(1) Passengers A wants to buy a gift for his wife. Help him to purchase the proper

duty-free goods.

(2) A passenger wants to buy a bottle of vodka but it is out of stock. How do you explain to the passenger?

Part Five   Exercise

1 Fill in the blanks in the following dialogues

Dialogue 1

PAX: Excuse me, Miss?

CA: Yes? _____(1)_____ (我能为您做点什么呢)?

PAX: Do you have any _____(2)_____ (免税商品)on board?

CA: Yes, sir. We have a wide selection of duty-free goods, such as _____(3)_____ (手表), spirits, _____(4)_____ (香水), cosmetics and so on. Here is the catalog.

PAX: Oh. This watch looks good. How much is it?

CA: It's 130 US dollars. You can try it on, sir.

PAX: OK. I will take it.

CA: _____(5)_____ (现金)or credit card, sir?

PAX: Here is my credit card.

CA: Thank you!

Dialogue 2

CA: Excuse me, madam? Are you interested in any duty-free goods?

PAX: I want to buy something for my daughter, I'm not sure _____(6)_____ (买点什么). Do you have any _____(7)_____ (推荐)?

CA: You can read the _____(8)_____ (机上免税商品杂志)here. How about some _____(9)_____ (巧克力)?

PAX: It looks _____(10)_____ (挺好). I'll take two bars.

2 Translate the following phrases into English

(1) 化妆品   (2) 珠宝

(3) 烈性酒   (4) 香烟

(5) 货币   (6) 现金

(7) 信用卡   (8) 折扣

(9) 伏特加   (10) 香水

3 Translate the following sentences into English

(1) 请问您用什么支付？

(2) 我们可以收取现金和信用卡。

(3) 如果您使用信用卡付款，我们还需要您的护照。

(4) 这是找给您的钱。

（5）您需要的香水已售完。

4 Translate the following sentences into Chinese

（1）The duty-free goods magazine is in the seat pocket.

（2）Would you like any duty-free goods, sir?

（3）Sorry, madam. Your card has expired.

（4）Please tell the cabin attendant if you need any help.

（5）I'm afraid that I can't give you any discount. All the items we sell on board are marked prices.

Part Six Supplementary Reading

Duty-free Service

In the aircraft on certain international flight, or at duty-free goods shops located in the waiting hall for international flights or in transit areas in airports, passengers can purchase some duty-free items. The purchase price of a duty-free item is exempt from the tax that is normally added by the country or city in which the sale is taking place. Thus, duty-free items are less expensive than items bought where the duty-free condition does not apply. By shopping duty-free items, 15% to 40% off the suggested retail price can be saved. The passengers can buy duty-free goods as gifts or souvenirs. Therefore, this duty-free service is welcomed by most of the international passengers.

Passengers can browse through the in-flight duty-free magazines located in the seat pocket in front of them, and then choose products they want to buy. In-flight duty-free goods are often made up of some of the most famous brands in the world, including electronic goods, confectioneries, perfume, skincare products, cosmetics, cigarettes, jewelry, spirits, watches, etc.

The cabin attendants from different airlines may provide duty-free service in almost the same procedures. Usually, the cabin attendants will make the announcement first for duty-free goods. The passengers can read the in-flight duty-free items from the magazines located in the seat pocket in front of them. And then they can choose duty-free items from the magazines by filling in the order forms. They may usually allow the passengers to choose about 30 minutes and go along the aisle to collect the forms. They will take the goods to the passengers. The goods can be paid by cash or most major credit cards, like Diners Club, Visa, Master Card, American Express, and so on.

Decide whether the following statements are true (T) or false (F) according to the passage

（1）In addition to the duty-free shops in the airport lounge, passengers can buy a range of duty-free items on international flights. (   )

（2）By shopping duty-free items, 15% to 30% off the suggested retail price can be saved. (   )

(3) The in-flight duty-free magazines are normally located in the seat pocket in front of the passengers. (   )

(4) The cabin attendants may usually allow the passengers to choose about 30 minutes. (   )

(5) The goods can be paid by cash or most major credit cards. (   )

Module 3 Special Situation

Unit 9 Serving Special Passengers

1. Be familiar with the types of special passengers.
2. Know how to serve different types of special passengers.
3. Grasp relevant English words and expressions.
4. Know the cabin attendants' responsibilities.

Part One Listening

1 Listen to the dialogue and choose the best answer to each question

(1) How much milk powder will be plenty to make 120 mL of milk for the baby?
A. Full spoon
B. 4 spoonfuls
C. 120 mL

(2) How to make milk powder correctly according to the dialogue?
A. Use hot water
B. Use water with the temperature above 40 degrees
C. Use water with the temperature about 40 degrees

听力音频

2 Listen to the dialogue and fill in the blanks

(A cabin attendant is welcoming passengers on board.)

CA: cabin attendant   PAX: passenger

CA: Good morning, sir. Welcome aboard!

PAX: Good morning. Could you help me manage my wheelchair, please?

CA: Certainly. _____(1)_____?

PAX: Of course. It could. I would not use it on board.

CA: Don't worry, sir. To make it convenient, we have cabin wheelchairs which are _____(2)_____ on our aircraft, and can be used by passengers _____(3)_____. Our flight attendants are all trained and _____(4)_____ in using the wheelchair.

PAX: That's great!

CA: _____(5)_____?

PAX: No. Thank you very much.

CA: My pleasure, sir. Wish you a pleasant trip!

Part Two Dialogues

CA: cabin attendant   PAX: passenger

1 Dialogue 1

(A lady presses the call button. A cabin attendant goes there to see what the matter is.)

CA: Good morning, madam. Did you press the call button? What can I do for you?

PAX: Oh, yes. I'm not feeling very well now.

CA: I'm sorry to hear that. What's the problem, madam?

PAX: I feel very tired and a little dizzy. I tried to sleep, but I can't fall asleep. It has been last for some hours. So, could you help me with it?

CA: Don't worry, madam. From my experience, maybe you are suffering from jet lag.

PAX: This is my first time flying over such a long distance. So, I have never experienced jet lag. Will it be serious?

CA: No, it will be fine. When we travel through several time zones, our body is slow to catch up with the change in time. Therefore, jet lag often leads to circadian disturbances in body function. But don't worry, please. This is very common.

PAX: OK, I know. Then what should I do?

CA: You'd better have a rest. And I will go to the front cabin to see if there are any empty seats. So, you can lie down and try to fall asleep. You will feel better then.

PAX: Thank you.

CA: It's my pleasure. Please feel free to call us if you have any other problems.

PAX: OK, I will.

2 Dialogue 2

(A cabin attendant called Lily is welcoming the passengers boarding in the cabin. She notices an old lady is coming toward her with bags in her hands. So she comes to help her.)

CA: Good morning, madam. Welcome aboard. May I help you with your bags?

PAX: Yes. It's very kind of you!

CA: It's my pleasure. What's your seat number, or may I have your boarding pass, please?

PAX: My seat number is 39C. This is my boarding pass.

CA: OK. Please follow me to your seat. (After they get to the seat.) Let me help you put your hand baggage in the overhead compartment. Please fasten the seat belt when you are seated. You can adjust the seat back by pressing the button on your armrest. But please be sure to return the seat back to the upright position when taking off or landing.

PAX: OK. I will.

CA: The lavatory is located in the front of the cabin. Since the air conditioner of this plane is a little strong, to keep warm, blankets are available for passengers if needed. Would you like one?

PAX: Yes, I'd like one. How considerate!

CA: It's my pleasure to serve you well. Is there anything I can do for you?

PAX: I'm a little thirsty. Could I have a cup of water?

CA: Sorry. Because the plane will take off quite shortly, the beverage couldn't be served now. I will bring you the water as soon as the take-off finishes. It won't be too long. Will a cup of warm water be OK for you, madam?

PAX: Yes, thank you for all you have done for me!

CA: It's my pleasure. Please press the call button on the overhead unit if you need anything for help.

PAX: OK!

3 Dialogue 3

(A cabin attendant named Ella stands at the cabin door to welcome passengers. A blind man is boarding with a guide dog.)

CA: Excuse me, sir. I'm the cabin attendant for this flight. Would you please show me your boarding pass?

PAX1: Sure, here you are. Thank you.

CA: It's 16C. Please give me your hand. I'll take you to your seat.

PAX1: Many thanks.

CA: You are welcome.

PAX1: How about my guide dog? Can it stay with me in the seat?

CA: Yes. The dog can sit at your feet.

PAX1: That's great!

(After they get to the seat.)

CA: Your baggage has been put into the overhead compartment. Let me help you fasten the seat belt. (Ella leads the man's hand to the button on the armrest.) And you could adjust the seat back by pressing the button on the side of your armrest.

Anything else I can do for you, sir?

PAX1: Yes. I'd like to take a nap after a while. I wonder if there are pillows and blankets on the flight?

CA: Sure. I will bring them for you soon. If you need any help, please don't hesitate to call me.

PAX1: Thanks.

CA: (To the passenger sitting next to the blind man.) Excuse me, sir. Would you like to help him press the call button if he needs my help?

PAX2: No problem.

CA: Thank you for your kindness.

PAX2: Don't mention it.

4 Dialogue 4

(A pregnant woman with baggage in hand is boarding the plane. A cabin attendant named Mary comes up to her.)

CA: Hello, madam. Welcome aboard.

PAX: Thank you.

CA: May I know your seat number? So I could show you there. And may I help you with your bags?

PAX: Sure, thank you. My seat number is 24D. It's really kind of you.

CA: You are welcome. Here is your seat. Let me help you put your bags into the overhead compartment. And before you fasten the seat belt, please allow me to bring a blanket for you. It may make you more comfortable and safer during the flight. Please wait a moment.

PAX: Thank you.

(A few minutes later, Mary returns to this lady.)

CA: Excuse me, madam. Here's your blanket. I suggest putting the blanket under the seat belt when it fastens.

PAX: Oh, I don't know how to put it. Could you help me with that?

CA: Sure. First, please fold the blanket to a suitable size. Next, put the blanket on your belly, and fasten the two ends of the seat belt to the root of your thighs outside of the blanket, so that your baby will feel more comfortable.

PAX: Yes, I feel better now. Thank you.

CA: It's my pleasure. I also bring some airsickness bags for you. If you feel sick, you may use them. They could be found in the seat pocket in front of you.

PAX: OK, I will.

CA: If you have any problems, please don't hesitate to call me during the flight. The call button is on the unit over your head.

PAX: I couldn't thank you more for what you have done for me.

CA: It's my duty to serve you well. Wish you enjoy the journey!

5 Words and expressions

dizzy [ˈdɪzi] *adj.* 头晕目眩的；眩晕的
jet lag 时差反应
time zone 时区
circadian B[sɜːˈkeɪdiən]/A[sɜːrˈkeɪdiən] *adj.* 昼夜节律的；生理节奏的
disturbance B[dɪˈstɜːbəns]/A[dɪˈstɜːrbəns] *n.*（受）打扰；干扰；妨碍；紊乱
lavatory B[ˈlævətri]/A[ˈlævətɔːri] *n.* 厕所；卫生间；盥洗室
air conditioner 空调设备
blanket [ˈblæŋkɪt] *n.* 毯子；毛毯
considerate [kənˈsɪdərət] *adj.* 考虑周到的
guide dog 导盲犬
nap [næp] *n.*（日间的）小睡；打盹
pillow B[ˈpɪləʊ]/A[ˈpɪloʊ] *n.* 枕头
pregnant [ˈpregnənt] *adj.* 怀孕的；妊娠的
belly [ˈbeli] *n.* 腹部；肚子
thigh [θaɪ] *n.* 大腿
airsickness bag 晕机袋

6 Notes to the dialogues

(1) From my experience, maybe you are suffering from jet lag.
根据我的经验，或许您有些时差反应。

(2) Therefore, jet lag often leads to circadian disturbances in body function.
因此，时差反应经常导致人体功能的昼夜节律紊乱。

(3) ...blankets are available for passengers if needed.
……如果需要的话，我们可以为旅客提供毛毯。

(4) ...put the blanket on your belly, and fasten the two ends of the seat belt to the root of your thighs outside of the blanket ...
……把毛毯盖在腹部，然后将安全带的两端固定在毛毯外侧大腿根部……

Part Three Announcements

1 Birthday greeting

Ladies and gentlemen,
　　Today is the birthday of Mr. / Mrs. /Miss ＿＿＿, seated in Row No. ＿＿＿. On behalf of ＿＿＿ Airlines, it is our great pleasure to offer birthday greetings to Mr. /Mrs. /Miss ＿＿＿ (and we have a gift for him /her).
　　To Mr. /Mrs. /Miss ＿＿＿, Happy Birthday!

广播音频

2 Upgrading

Ladies and gentlemen,

We are pleased to inform you that we have some First Class (and Business Class) seats available on our flight today. If you desire to upgrade, we will be pleased to assist you.

Thank you!

3 Festival greeting

Good morning (afternoon/ evening), ladies and gentlemen,

This is your (chief) purser speaking. It is Spring Festival, Chinese Lunar New Year day, on behalf of _____ Airlines, the entire crew here extend sincere greetings to you. We wish you good health, a happy and prosperous New Year!

Thank you!

4 Words and phrases

Spring Festival 春节
lunar B['luːnə(r)]/A['luːnər] *adj*. 月球的；月亮的；阴历的
prosperous B['prɒspərəs]/A['prɑːspərəs] *adj*. 繁荣的；兴旺的

Part Four Role Play

In small groups, make up a dialogue based on the following situations

(1) An old man is boarding the plane. Please help him to find his seat and tell the instructions before taking off.

(2) A blind passenger is boarding with a guide dog. She needs someone to help her boarding.

Part Five Exercise

1 Fill in the blanks in the following dialogues

Dialogue 1

CA: Excuse me, sir. _____(1)_____ (请出示一下您的登机牌好吗)?

PAX1: Sure, here you are.

CA: It's 16C. Please give me your hand. _____(2)_____ (我带您去您的座位).

PAX1: Many thanks.

CA: You are welcome. (After they get to the seat.) _____(3)_____ (您的行李已经放到行李架了). Let me help you fasten the seat belt. _____(4)_____ (还有

其他事情可以帮您吗)?

PAX：No, thanks.

CA：(To the passenger sitting next to the blind man.) Excuse me, sir. ＿＿＿＿＿＿(5)＿＿＿＿＿＿(如果他有任何事情需要帮助,请帮他按一下呼唤铃好吗)?

PAX2：No problem.

CA：Thank you for your kindness.

Dialogue 2

CA：Good morning, madam. Welcome aboard. ＿＿＿＿＿(6)＿＿＿＿＿(需要我帮您提一下行李吗)?

PAX：Yes. It's very kind of you!

CA：It's my pleasure. What's your seat number, please?

PAX：My seat number is 39C.

CA：OK. ＿＿＿＿(7)＿＿＿＿(请跟随我到您的座位). Let me help you put your hand baggage into the overhead compartment. ＿＿＿＿＿(8)＿＿＿＿＿(落座后,请系好安全带).

PAX：OK. I will.

CA：Since the air conditioner of this plane is a little strong, ＿＿＿＿＿(9)＿＿＿＿＿(为了保暖,我们可以为您提供毛毯). Would you like one?

PAX：Yes, I'd like one. How considerate!

CA：＿＿＿＿＿(10)＿＿＿＿＿(为您提供优质服务是我应尽的职责). Is there anything else I can do for you?

PAX：No, thank you!

2 Translate the following phrases into English

(1) 时差反应　　　　　　(2) 时区
(3) 空调　　　　　　　　(4) 毛毯
(5) 枕头　　　　　　　　(6) 导盲犬
(7) 怀孕的　　　　　　　(8) 小睡

3 Translate the following sentences into English

(1) 根据我的经验,或许您有些时差反应。
(2) 当我们穿越时区时,我们的身体很难及时跟上时间的变化。
(3) 我去前舱看看是否还有空余座位。
(4) 请将安全带的两端固定在毛毯外侧大腿根部。
(5) 晕机袋就放在您前排座椅的口袋中。

4 Translate the following sentences into Chinese

(1) Jet lag often leads to circadian disturbances in body function.
(2) Please feel free to call us if you have any other problems.
(3) You can adjust the seat back by pressing the button on your armrest.

(4) Because the plane will take off quite shortly, the beverage couldn't be served now.

(5) On behalf of our airlines, it is my great pleasure to offer birthday greetings to Mr. Smith.

Part Six Supplementary Reading

Unaccompanied Minor

Unaccompanied Minor (short for UM), refers to a child passenger who is over 5 years old but under 12 years old on the date of the start of air transportation, and is not accompanied by an adult over 18 years old on the plane.

Usually, children take flights with their parents together. However, many parents are busy with work and cannot pick up and drop off their children every time. So, airlines provide flight services for unaccompanied children, allowing children to fly alone without parents, worrying about the security.

First, unaccompanied child should be accompanied by the child's parent or guardian to the airport, and the ground staff will take care of the child's boarding and disembarkation. The name, address and contact phone number of the person who is responsible for drop-off and pick-up should be provided to the airlines.

Most airlines only accept the transportation of unaccompanied children without connecting flights. When the entire voyage of transportation includes two or more flight arrangements, whether it is carried by the same carrier or by different carriers, the child's parent or guardian should arrange for personnel to pick up and take care of the child during the transit.

Since the airlines are responsible for unaccompanied children and need to provide special services and care, there should be a certain limit on the number of unaccompanied children carried on each flight. For example, China Eastern Airlines requires that no more than 4 unaccompanied children could be carried on the B767 airplane. China Southern Airlines requires that no more than 10 unaccompanied children could be carried on the A380 airplane, and only economy class accepts unaccompanied children, not in first class and business class.

When checking in, the airport will issue a bag with "Unaccompanied" identification for the child, and the child must wear it during the whole flight. All the relevant documents of the child are placed in the "Unaccompanied" bag. When the check-in finished, the unaccompanied child will be handed over to the airport ground staff. The ground staff will lead the child through the security check, and send the child on the plane to the flight attendant. After boarding the plane, one certain flight attendant will be required to take care of the child. She will tell the child to press the call button when he or she needs help. If the child can't reach it, he can ask nearby passengers for help. If passengers need to take the shuttle bus when get off the plane, the child needs to take the bus by himself. After getting off the shuttle bus, there will be a ground staff picking up the child, helping with the luggage and sending the child to the exit.

Even though it is very common for a child to take a flight alone, security is always the most important. Just remember to remind the child that, in any case, when he or she is puzzled or meets difficulties, find the staff for help as soon as possible.

Decide whether the following statements are true (T) or false (F) according to the passage

(1) Unaccompanied Minor refers to a child passenger who is over 5 years old but under 18 years old on the date of the start of air transportation. (   )

(2) The children's parents or guardian have to help the children boarding and pick up the children on the plane when they disembark. (   )

(3) Most airlines only accept the transportation of unaccompanied children with direct flights. (   )

(4) The unaccompanied children must wear the "unaccompanied" bag during the whole flight. (   )

(5) There are no limits on the number of unaccompanied children carried on each flight. (   )

Unit 10　Lost Baggage

Learning Objectives

1. Be familiar with various boarding dialogues and announcements.
2. Grasp relevant English expressions.
3. Know how to give announcements when some passengers lose their baggage.
4. Know how to deal with the situation when some passengers lose their baggage.

Part One　Listening

1　Listen to the dialogue and choose the best answer to each question

(1) What's the matter with the woman?
A. She cannot find her watch.
B. She cannot find her seat.
C. She wants to go to the lavatory.

听力音频

(2) Where did the woman find her lost item?

A. Under her seat

B. In the lavatory

C. At the cabin door

2 Listen to the dialogue and fill in the blanks

(A passenger looks very worried. He lost his handbag and comes to a flight attendant.)

PAX: Excuse me, Miss. I've lost my _____(1)_____.

CA: I'm sorry to hear that. Are you sure you've lost it in the cabin?

PAX: Yes, I've looked for it everywhere but found nothing.

CA: Perhaps it is under your seat or in the _____(2)_____.

PAX: No.

CA: Are there any _____(3)_____ in it?

PAX: No, just a few dollars. But there are some important documents in it. That's why I'm really worried about it.

CA: Please remain calm and think about when and where you lost it.

PAX: I remember I had it when I was in the waiting room. But when I got into the cabin, I didn't have it. I'm not sure where I lost it. Maybe I left it in the waiting room.

CA: Well. Please leave your name, _____(4)_____, telephone number and any other details about your handbag.

PAX: Of course. Here you are.

CA: All right. I'll report to the _____(5)_____ immediately. He'll send the message to the ground staff. If we find it, we will send it over to you.

PAX: Thank you for your help.

Part two Dialogues

CA: cabin attendant   PAX: passenger

1 Dialogue 1

对话音频

(A passenger lost his handbag.)

CA: May I help you?

PAX: I can't find my handbag.

CA: Is it in the overhead compartment or under the seat?

PAX: No, I have looked for it everywhere and found nothing.

CA: Did you have valuable things in it?

PAX: No. But there are some important files in it.

CA: Maybe you lost it in the airport. We'll now contact our ground staff to look for it. Could you please give us your name, home address, and a description of your handbag?

PAX: All right. Here you are.

CA: Is there anything particular?

PAX: Yes, there is a book, my ID card and two tickets for Sunday night's concert in my handbag.

CA: Don't worry. If there is any information about it, we'll contact you.

PAX: Thanks a lot.

2 Dialogue 2

CA: Can I help you, sir?

PAX1: I couldn't find my mobile phone when I woke up. I can't remember where I lost it. Maybe it slipped out of my pocket somewhere in the cabin. Nowadays, mobile phones are very important to every one. What should I do?

CA: Are you sure you lost it in the cabin?

PAX1: Yes, absolutely sure!

CA: Well, don't worry about it. We'll make an announcement to help you find it. Please wait for a moment.

PAX1: Thanks.

(Announcement: Ladies and gentlemen, a passenger has lost his mobile phone on board. If anyone has found it, please contact the cabin attendant by pressing the call button. Thank you!)

PAX2: (She presses the call button and talks to the CA.) Excuse me. I found a mobile phone on row 27. Here you are.

CA: Thank you, Miss. What's your name?

PAX2: Never mind. I did what I should do.

CA: (The cabin attendant goes to the passenger who lost his mobile phone.) Sir, what does your mobile phone look like? And what brand is it?

PAX1: It's a black iPhone X.

CA: Is this yours? It was found on row 27.

PAX1: Oh, yes, it's mine. Maybe I lost it when I talked to my friend.

CA: OK. Could you please sign here for confirmation?

PAX1: Sure. Thank you for your help.

CA: You are welcome.

3 Dialogue 3

(A passenger forgot her overcoat in the waiting room.)

PAX: (A passenger presses the call button and a cabin attendant comes up.)

CA: May I help you?

PAX: Miss, I've left my overcoat in the waiting room. I know where it is. Can I go and fetch it?

CA: Just a moment. I'll ask the permission of our chief purser. You may go now. Please hurry.

(After take-off.)

PAX: Oh, no! I can't find my glasses.

CA: Are you sure you've taken them on board?

PAX: Yes, but I couldn't find them there.

CA: What is the color of your glasses?

PAX: They're sun glasses with a black frame.

CA: Miss, your glasses have been found under the seat behind you. They must have dropped on the floor and slipped backwards during take-off.

PAX: Thank you for your help.

CA: You are welcome. Please take good care of your belongings.

4 Dialogue 4

PAX: Excuse me, Miss!

Ca: Yes, how can I help you?

PAX: I've lost one of my handbags.

CA: I'm sorry to hear that. When do you think you lost it?

PAX: I'm not sure. But I still had it when I went through the security check.

CA: Don't worry. Did you go shopping at DFS?

PAX: No. But I went to the restaurant near DFS. Then I went to the restroom in the waiting room.

CA: I see. I think you may have lost your bag in the restaurant or the restroom.

PAX: Can you help me to get it back?

CA: What is the color of your bag?

PAX: It's a dark green one.

CA: Do you remember what's in the bag?

PAX: Yes. There are some tens of dollars, a passport, a cell phone with a charger and a pack of cigarettes. When can I get it back?

CA: We'll try our best. We will ask our captain to inform the ground staff to look for it. If we find your bag, we will bring it to you on time.

PAX: Thanks. It's very kind of you.

5 Dialogue 5

(After take-off.)

CA: Hello sir, what can I do for you?

PAX: It is really terrible. I just can't find one of my handbags. What can I do about it?

CA: Are you sure you've taken them on board?

PAX: No, I'm not sure. Maybe I forgot it in the waiting room.

CA: Don't worry too much about it. We'll try to find it for you. Would you show me your boarding card and baggage check, please?

PAX: OK.

CA: Thanks. Could you describe your handbag?

PAX: It is not big, made of cloth and red.

CA: What about the size?

PAX: About 30 by 20 by 15 centimeters.

CA: Please fill in this form, leave your home address and telephone number.

PAX: All right. But should I complete all the sections?

CA: Yes, you should. Especially make your address and contact phone number in Beijing clear, so we can contact you easily.

PAX: I have completed the form. Here you are.

CA: Thank you. If we find it, we will send it over to you.

PAX: Thank you, but I hope you are determined to find it for me.

CA: Yes, we are. You can rely on us.

6 Words and expressions

address B[əˈdres]/A[ˈædres] v. 写(收信人)姓名地址;致函;演说 n. 住址;地址;通信处

description [dɪˈskrɪpʃn] n. 描写(文字);形容;说明

particular B[pəˈtɪkjələ(r)]/A[pərˈtɪkjələr] n. (正式记下的)细节;详情;详细资料

concert B[ˈkɒnsət]/A[ˈkɑːnsərt] n. 音乐会;演奏会

absolutely [ˈæbsəluːtli] adv. 绝对地;完全地

brand B[brænd]/A[brænd] n. 品牌;类型

confirmation B[ˌkɒnfəˈmeɪʃn]A[ˌkɑːnfərˈmeɪʃn] n. 证实;确认书

fetch [fetʃ] v. (去)拿来;(去)请来

permission B[pəˈmɪʃn]/A[pərˈmɪʃn] n. 准许;许可

chief purse 主任乘务长

frame [freɪm] n. 框架 v. 给……做框;给……镶边

belongings B[bɪˈlɒŋɪŋz]/A[bɪˈlɔːŋɪŋz] n. 动产;财物

security check 安全检查

cigarette B[ˌsɪɡəˈret]/A[ˈsɪɡəret] n. 香烟

centimeter B[ˈsentɪˌmiːtə]/A[ˈsentəˌmiːtər] n. 厘米

determined B[dɪˈtɜːmɪnd]/A[dɪˈtɜːrmɪnd] adj. 坚定的;坚决的;果断的

7 Notes to the dialogues

(1) Could you please give us your name, home address, and a description of your handbag?

您可以留下您的姓名、地址、电话号码和有关您手提包的细节吗？

(2) Maybe it slipped out of my pocket somewhere in the cabin.

也许它从我口袋里掉出来,掉在客舱的某个地方了。

(3) Could you please sign here for confirmation?

能麻烦您在这签字确认吗？

(4) I'll ask the permission of our chief purser.

我去问一下主任乘务长。

(5) Miss, your glasses have been found under the seat behind you. They must have dropped on the floor and slipped backwards during take-off.

女士,您的眼镜已经在您后排座位下找到了,一定是飞机起飞时掉落滑到后面去了。

(6) DFS：Duty Free Shop

免税店

(7) We will ask our captain to inform the ground staff to look for it.

我们会立刻向机长报告,他会通知机场工作人员帮您寻找。

(8) send it over

送过去

(9) rely on

信任

Part Three　Announcements

1　Lost and found

广播音频

Ladies and gentlemen,

May I have your attention, please? If there is a passenger who has lost a mobile phone in the cabin, please notify the cabin attendant by pressing the call button.

Thank you!

2　Lost and found

Ladies and gentlemen,

May I have your attention, please? One of the passengers found a wallet in the cabin and handed it over to us. The passenger who has lost it, please come to the front galley to claim it.

Thank you!

3　Lost and found

Ladies and gentlemen,

May I have your attention, please? A handbag was found in the waiting room in the terminal building. If there is a passenger who has lost it, please identify yourself to the cabin attendant immediately.

Thank you!

4 Lost and found

Ladies and gentlemen,

May I have your attention, please? One of the passengers who had lost her sun glasses in the cabin. If anyone has found it, please contact us by pressing the call button. Thank you!

5 Words and phrases

notify B['nəʊtɪfaɪ]/A['noʊtɪfaɪ] v. 通知
identify [aɪ'dentɪfaɪ] v. 确认身份

6 Notes to the announcements

hand it over 移交

Part Four Role Play

In small groups, make up a dialogue based on the following situations

(1) A woman leaves her handbag at the security counter. She's got an ipad and some clothes in it. After contacting the ground staff, her handbag is sent back before the cabin door is closed.

(2) A passenger cannot find his mobile phone. He is sure the mobile phone was lost in the cabin. Make an announcement to ask for other passengers' help. Another passenger finds it in the lavatory.

Part Five Exercise

1 Fill in the blanks in the following dialogues

Dialogue 1

PAX: Excuse me, Miss. I was wondering if you could help me.

CA: Yes, sir.

PAX: I forgot to pick up my briefcase. I think _____(1)_____ it in the departure lounge at the airport.

CA: Would you please _____(2)_____ it so that we can _____(3)_____ it for you.

PAX: Well, it's a normal size, black leather, executive _____(4)_____. It has my _____(5)_____ in it _____(6)_____ Arthur Hudson. It also has my _____(7)_____ in Seattle. There are some important business papers in it. I'm a bit worried.

CA：Are you sure you left it in the lounge?

PAX：Yes … I'm sure. I left it at _____(8)_____. I had just bought a pack of cigarettes there.

CA：OK. We'll try to find it for you. Would you please give me _____(9)_____ of the hotel where you're going to stay?

PAX：I'll be staying at Jinghua Hotel for a week.

CA：We'll _____(10)_____ you as soon as we find your briefcase.

PAX：Thank you very much.

Dialogue 2

PAX：Excuse me. _____(11)_____（我何时能拿回我的手提包）?

CA：It is hard to say, Miss. We'll try our best to contact our ground staff. It will take them some time to look for your handbag.

PAX：_____(12)_____（他们能帮我找到吗）?

CA：_____(13)_____（目前还无法确切回答您需要多久才能找回您的手提包）. We'll help you to look for your lost property. If it is found, we'll contact you immediately.

PAX：It's so kind of you.

2 Translate the following phrases into English

(1) 安全检查   (2) 重要文件

(3) 候机厅   (4) 主任乘务长

(5) 失物招领   (6) 通知

(7) 钱包   (8) 移交

(9) 音乐会   (10) 演奏会

3 Translate the following sentences into English

(1) 您确定您的手提包是在客舱遗失的吗？

(2) 您可以提供您的姓名、住址、手机号码和手提包的详细情况吗？

(3) 如果有任何消息，我们会立即与您取得联系。

(4) 如果有旅客在机上捡到这个钱包，请按呼叫按钮联系乘务员。

(5) 我会立即向机长报告，他会发信息给机场工作人员。

4 Translate the following sentences into Chinese

(1) Can you describe your baggage?

(2) I think you may have lost your handbag in the waiting hall.

(3) Once your baggage has been found, they will contact you to arrange the delivery.

(4) It is hard to say when we will find your handbag, Miss. But we'll try our best to contact the ground staff. It will take them some time to look for your handbag.

(5) You need to complete an irregularity report form. Make sure all the blanks are filled out.

5 Fill in the Lost Property Report based on the following information

Tom Hardy was taking the Delta flight DL1977 from Washington DC to Los Angeles on April 5, 2020. He lost his dark brown briefcase before he boarded the plane. He was sure to have his briefcase when he was in the waiting hall. Then he went to a food court and a few shops. He's got some important documents and a few dollars in his briefcase. He is worried. His phone number is 8554463982. His email address is TH323@gmail.com.

Lost Property Report
LOST PROPERTY INQUIRY START
Property Lost
(1) Maximum allowed: 50characters

(2) Possible location where your item was lost (select all that apply) *

Airline Terminal/Gate	Airline Lounge	Airport Food Court	Airport Restaurants
Airport Hotel	Airport Shops	Airport Bathrooms	On the Airplane
Connecting Flight	Security Check In	Parking Garage	Taxi Transport
Bus Transport	Train Transport	Baggage Claim	Do Not Know

AIRPORT / AIRLINE / FLIGHT DETAILS
Country: (3)　　　Airline: (4)　　　Flight number: (5)
CONTACT INFORMATION
Name: (6)
Email Address: (7)
Phone (Home, Cell, or International): (8)
INCIDENT DETAILS
Lost Date: Month (9)　　　Day (10)　　　Year (11)
Detailed description of the lost property
(12)

Part Six　Supplementary Reading

The Liability of the Air Carrier in Tracing Baggage

We apologize for the mishandling of your baggage and understand that this will be inconvenient for you. Please be assured that we will do everything to help you through this situation. Your baggage details have been entered into our worldwide computerized baggage tracing system. If any of your information has changed, or if after reviewing your file you have corrections, it would be appreciated if you could notify us immediately so we can update your file accordingly. It would also be most helpful if you could ensure your name, address and baggage description are correct. This will help us in returning your baggage to you quickly.

In case of a misdirected bag, the Baggage Service Office is responsible for the tracing process for the first five days. It is important that you report the loss immediately after arriving at the airport. Most of the misdirected baggage can be found within 24 hours. In the rare cases when missing baggage is not found within the first five days, a second more detailed tracing process begins. For this reason, we ask you to provide us with as many details about the baggage items as possible.

If the airline is unable to find your lost baggage and declares it lost, the compensation process is activated. According to IATA guidelines, passengers are entitled to claim with maximum liability of the airline being limited to 20 US dollars per kilogram or a maximum of 635 US dollars per piece of the checked-in baggage.

Any damage to the baggage should be reported to the concerned airline immediately, within 24 hours of arrival at the airport. In case of the travel being made through a combination of various airline alliance partners, the delivering carrier is held responsible.

Ensure Your Baggage Safety

There are two possible factors that can make you lose your baggage. One is the airline's fault, the other one is a fellow passenger's fault because of the identical appearance of the baggage. To avoid it from happening, the best way to avoid lost baggage is to carry it on, but that's getting ridiculously hard with new airport rules (checking is now expensive). Before checking a bag(leaving a bag when you check in which then goes in the plane's cargo hold), label it inside and out. Label bags are only a little helpful to the folks looking for your lost baggage, but very helpful when you need to claim them. Label all your baggage with name label which gives your address, telephone number etc. Lock all the bags and remove old destination and identification tags before checking baggage. Never put cash, jewellery, electronic equipment, computers in the checked-in baggage, as airlines will not be liable for any loss or damage. Take a picture of your baggage, preferably with a color tag, and store it in the phone's camera or in a digital camera. Print it out and keep it with your passport in your carry on. If you have to report a missing bag, you have an easy way to show the ground staff what your baggage looks like.

Decide whether the following statements are true (T) or false (F) according to the passage

(1) After you checked in, your baggage details have been entered into the worldwide computerized baggage tracing system. (   )

(2) Most misdirected baggage can be found within 48 hours. (   )

(3) If the baggage is declared lost, the maximum liability of the airline is 20 US

dollars per piece. (   )

(4) In order to avoid the possibility of losing baggage, the best way is to take a picture. (   )

(5) It is reasonable to put cash, jewelry, electronic equipment, computer in the check-in baggage. (   )

Unit 11   Flight Delay

Learning Objectives

1. Be familiar with the reasons for flight delay.
2. Know how to explain the delay to passengers.
3. Grasp some English words and expressions concerned.
4. Know the cabin attendants' responsibilities.

Part One   Listening

1 Listen to the dialogue, and choose the best answer to each question

(1) Why has the plane been delayed?
A. Because of the fog
B. Because of the smog
C. Because of the airport

(2) When does the passenger have to get to Shanghai?
A. Before tomorrow
B. Before this evening
C. Before this afternoon

2 Listen to the dialogue and fill in the blanks

(A cabin attendant is welcoming passengers on board.)

CA: cabin attendant   PAX: passenger

PAX: Excuse me. It's 10:30 a. m. now, and half an hour later than _____(1)_____ . Why has our plane not taken off?

CA: _____(2)_____ , madam. We have just received the news from ground staff that there is _____(3)_____ with the plane.

听力音频

PAX: That's too bad. When will we take off?
CA: I understand how you feel, but we have to ＿＿＿＿(4)＿＿＿＿.
PAX: OK. Hopefully it won't take long.
CA: ＿＿＿＿(5)＿＿＿＿.

Part Two Dialogues

AC: airport crew   CA: cabin attendant   PAX: passenger

1 Dialogue 1

(A passenger is waiting to board in the airport. It has been 20 minutes later than the boarding time on his ticket, so he asks an airport crew for the reasons.)

PAX: Excuse me, Miss. It has been 9:40 a.m. Why haven't we boarded the plane?
AC: Good morning, sir. Which flight do you take?
PAX: My flight number is CA1032.
AC: Let me see ... Yes, it's not yet time to board this flight.
PAX: I wonder why my ticket says the boarding time is 9:20 a.m. It has been 20 minutes delayed now.
AC: I'm sorry for the delay, sir. Your flight is a connecting flight. The latest news shows that your flight was delayed for one hour when it departed from Dalian due to bad weather. Therefore, the arrival of this flight will be delayed by approximately one hour. Please wait patiently.
PAX: Oh, my god. It's too bad. So, I can only wait here?
AC: Yes. If there is further news, we will let you know as soon as possible.
PAX: OK, thanks a lot.

2 Dialogue 2

(A passenger is waiting for take-off in the cabin. It has been 15 minutes past the departure time, so he presses the call button.)

PAX: Excuse me, Miss. It has been 15 minutes past the scheduled departure time on my boarding pass. Why our plane hasn't taken off yet?
CA: Sorry, sir. According to the regulations of CAAC, the departure time on boarding pass refers to the time for closing cabin doors, but not for take-off.
PAX: Oh, I see. But when can we take off?
CA: The air traffic is very busy today. We have to wait for the plane ahead of us to take off first.
PAX: Do I have to wait a long time?
CA: I don't think it will take too long. And I appreciate your patient waiting.
PAX: OK. I will.
CA: Thank you for your cooperation.

3 Dialogue 3

(The flight was delayed. A passenger asks a cabin attendant for the reasons.)

PAX: Excuse me? May I ask you a question?

CA: Yes, please.

PAX: I'm wondering why our plane hasn't taken off yet. It has been half an hour late. Is it delayed?

CA: Yes, I apologize for the delay. There is heavy fog over Beijing airport. So, we can't take off now.

PAX: Why can't we take off?

CA: The visibility over the airport is much lower than the standard required by CAAC. It could be very dangerous if we take off now. I really apologize for having kept you waiting for such a long time.

PAX: Then how long will we wait?

CA: We haven't got the exact time for departure at present. And we have to wait until the weather gets better. I don't think it will take too long.

PAX: It's really terrible!

CA: I apologize for the inconvenience brought to you.

PAX: That's OK. It's not your fault.

CA: Thank you for your understanding.

4 Dialogue 4

(A passenger just heard an announcement that his flight would be delayed, so he asked a cabin attendant for the reasons.)

PAX: Excuse me. Just now I heard the announcement that this flight has been delayed.

CA: Yes. It has been delayed. The delay is due to some mechanical troubles. The engineers are taking a careful examination of our aircraft.

PAX: Is it serious? How long are we going to wait?

Ca: We are not sure about the time for take-off. But don't worry. You will be informed when the troubles are solved.

PAX: OK. Thanks a lot.

(15 minutes later, the flight still doesn't take off. The passenger asks the cabin attendant again.)

PAX: Hi, Miss. Another 15 minutes have passed. Haven't the troubles been solved yet?

CA: I'm awfully sorry for having kept you waiting for such a long time. The ground staff says it might be finished in 10 minutes. So, please wait a moment.

PAX: I hope the plane will take off shortly, or I will be late for my connecting flight.

CA: May I know the departure time of your connecting flight?

PAX: The departure time is 11:20 a.m. If we arrive there on schedule, there is one hour left for me to transfer.

CA: Don't worry, sir. If you miss the flight, you could go to the transit counter and they will make a new arrangement for you.

PAX: Anyway, I hope our flight will take off soon.

CA: I hope so, too. Sorry for any inconvenience.

5 Words and expressions

boarding time 登机时间

delay [dɪˈleɪ] *n.* 延误;延期;耽搁 *v.* 延误;延迟;推迟;使迟到

connecting flight 转接班机;换乘班机

approximately B[əˈprɒksɪmətli]/A[əˈprɑːksɪmətli] *adv.* 大概;大约

schedule B[ˈʃedjuːl] /A[ˈskedʒuːl] *n.* 日程安排;时间表 *v.* 安排,为……安排时间

regulation [ˌregjuˈleɪʃn] *n.* 规章;制度;规则

CAAC *abbr.* 中国民用航空局(Civil Aviation Administration of China)

inconvenience [ˌɪnkənˈviːniəns] *n.* 不便;麻烦

mechanical [məˈkænɪkl] *adj.* 机械的;机器的

transfer [trænsˈfɜː(r)] *v.* 中转;换乘;(使)转移

transit [ˈtrænzɪt] *n.* 过境

transit counter 中转(过境)柜台

6 Notes to the dialogues

(1) ...your flight was delayed for one hour when it departed from Dalian due to bad weather.

……由于恶劣天气,您从大连出发的航班延迟了一个小时。

(2) According to the regulations of CAAC, the departure time on boarding pass refers to the time for closing cabin doors, but not for take-off.

根据中国民用航空局的规定,登机牌的起飞时间是指关闭机舱门的时间,而不是起飞时间。

(3) The visibility over the airport is much lower than the standard required by CAAC.

机场的能见度远低于中国民用航空局要求的能见度标准。

Part Three   Announcements

1 Brief delay departure

Ladies and gentlemen,

May I have your attention, please? This is your (chief) purser speaking. On behalf of _____ Airlines, we sincerely apologize for the delay in departure due to _____ (aircraft late arrival/air traffic control/unfavorable weather conditions/de-icing/mechanical troubles/cargo loading/airport congestion/waiting for some passengers).

广播音频

Please wait for a moment until we have further information for you.

We thank you for your patience and cooperation.

2 Delay due to weather conditions

Ladies and Gentlemen,

Attention, please. This is the purser speaking. Due to the _____ (snow storm/heavy fog/typhoon/thunderstorm/sandstorm), We will delay for take-off/have a further delay. Please remain seated and we will keep you updated. (During this period, the in-flight entertainment system is on. / We will provide the beverage/meal service.)

Thank you for your support and understanding.

3 Problems solved

Ladies and gentlemen,

With the excellent work of our airport crew, the mechanical trouble was solved. We have received take-off clearance from the ATC Tower. Our plane will depart in 10 minutes. Please confirm your seat belt is securely fastened and get ready for a safe take-off.

We sincerely apologize for the delay in departure and appreciate your understanding.

4 Wait in the terminal

Ladies and gentlemen,

We are informed that our flight will be delayed because of _____ (poor weather conditions /mechanical trouble). We ask that you wait in the terminal. Please take your ticket and boarding pass, and disembark. Your carry-on baggage may be left on board, but be sure to carry the valuables with you. Our ground staff will keep you informed of the latest information.

Thank you for your understanding and cooperation.

5 Words and phrases

de-icing [ˌdiːˈaɪsɪŋ] n. 除冰；融冰

cargo B[ˈkɑːɡəʊ]/A[ˈkɑːrɡoʊ] n. (船或飞机装载的)货物

congestion [kənˈdʒestʃən] n. (交通)拥塞；塞车

typhoon [taɪˈfuːn] n. 台风

thunderstorm B[ˈθʌndəstɔːm]/A[ˈθʌndərstɔːrm] n. 雷雨；雷暴

sandstorm B[ˈsændstɔːm]/A[ˈsændstɔːrm] n. 沙暴

ATC abbr. 空中交通管制(Air Traffic Control)

terminal B[ˈtɜːmɪnl]/A[ˈtɜːrmɪnl] n. 航空站

Part Four   Role play

In small groups, make up a dialogue based on the following situations.

(1) The flight was delayed due to the bad weather. Please comfort the passenger in the cabin.

(2) A passenger is worrying about the delay because it will make him miss his connecting flight. You are required to solve his problem.

Part Five   Exercise

1 Fill in the blanks in the following dialogues

Dialogue 1

PAX: Excuse me, Miss. It has been 20 minutes past the departure time on boarding pass. Why our plane hasn't taken off yet?

CA: Sorry, sir. According to the regulations of CAAC, ＿＿＿＿＿(1)＿＿＿＿＿（登机牌的起飞时间是指关闭机舱门的时间）, but not for take-off.

PAX: Oh, I see. But when can we take off?

CA: The air traffic is very busy today. ＿＿＿＿＿(2)＿＿＿＿＿（我们需要等待前面的飞机先行起飞）.

PAX: Do I have to wait a long time?

CA: I don't think it will take too long. ＿＿＿＿＿(3)＿＿＿＿＿（感谢您的耐心等候）.

PAX: OK. I will.

CA: ＿＿＿＿＿(4)＿＿＿＿＿（谢谢您的配合）.

Dialogue 2

PAX: I wonder why our plane hasn't taken off yet. Is it delayed?

CA: Yes, ＿＿＿＿＿(5)＿＿＿＿＿（我对此次延误致歉）. There is heavy fog over Nanjing airport. So, we can't take off now.

PAX: Why can't we take off?

CA: ＿＿＿＿＿(6)＿＿＿＿＿（机场的能见度远低于中国民用航空局规定的能见度标准）. It could be very dangerous if we take off now. ＿＿＿＿＿(7)＿＿＿＿＿（非常抱歉让您久等了）.

PAX: Then how long will we wait?

CA: ＿＿＿＿＿(8)＿＿＿＿＿（目前我们还未得到确切的起飞时间）. I don't think it will take too long.

PAX: It's really terrible!

CA: ＿＿＿＿＿(9)＿＿＿＿＿（给您带来的诸多不便,我们深表歉意）.

PAX: That's OK. It's not your fault.

2 Translate the following phrases into English

(1) 登机时间　　　　　　　　　　(2) 延误
(3) 转接班机　　　　　　　　　　(4) 时间安排
(5) 机械故障　　　　　　　　　　(6) 空中交通管制
(7) 中转柜台　　　　　　　　　　(8) 航站楼
(9) 货物装载　　　　　　　　　　(10) 大雾

3 Translate the following sentences into English

(1) 我的机票显示登机时间是下午3:20。
(2) 由于天气原因,我们的航班可能会延误一个小时。
(3) 如果有更进一步的消息,我们将尽快通知您。
(4) 此次延误是一些机械故障造成的。
(5) 如果错过转接航班,您可以去中转柜台安排新的行程。

4 Translate the following sentences into Chinese

(1) The arrival of this flight will be delayed by approximately one hour.
(2) You will be informed when the troubles are solved.
(3) The air traffic is very busy today.
(4) We have to wait until the weather gets better.
(5) We are not sure about the time for take-off.

Part Six Supplementary Reading

Flight Delay

Flight delay usually affects the operating efficiency and service quality of airlines. Generally, flight delay refers to the situation that the arrival time of one flight is more than 15 minutes later than the scheduled arrival time, or even the flight is cancelled.

There are certain events entirely beyond your control which could impact your flight. The flight could be delayed due to one of the following reasons.

Weather Reason

Weather is the main cause of flight delays. Generally, passengers do not know the specific bad weather that affected the flight. From the perspective of passengers, bad weather might mean heavy snow, heavy rain or heavy fog, etc. However, this understanding is inaccurate in fact. Here is an official explanation of the delay caused by bad weather from CAAC. Weather reason means that the flight fails to meet the flying standard due to weather conditions and therefore cannot take off on time. This includes many situations, i.e. the weather at the departure airport is not suitable for take-off; the weather at the destination airport is not suitable for landing; the weather on the flight route is not suitable for overflight, etc.

Air Traffic Control

The main impact of air traffic control on a flight is flow control. With the rapid development of civil aviation, the number of flights has been increasing sharply. However, the ground facilities, navigation equipment, and service support develops relatively slowly. They are unable to adapt to the current high-speed development of the civil aviation industry. In particular, due to reasons such as ensuring national defense security, our country has imposed strict airspace restrictions. The military is responsible for organizing and implementing national flight control tasks, so there is little room left for civil aviation in air traffic control.

Mechanical Troubles

Sometimes, before passengers board the plane or after boarding the plane, mechanical troubles are found. So, they have to wait in the cabin or even disembark and wait in the terminals. Once an aircraft breaks down during flight mission, the engineering staff will conduct necessary inspections, make judgments, find the reasons, and then carry out corresponding troubleshooting work in accordance with the procedures. Generally speaking, if mechanical troubles happen in the airline's base, it won't take too much time for the crew to handle the failure.

Passenger reason

There are many reasons for flight delays, many of which are caused by passengers themselves. Some passengers arrive at the airport quite late and even after the flight check-in deadline. For the convenience of passengers, airports and airlines will try their best to help these late passengers catch up with the flight smoothly, but this will inevitably cause the delay of the flight. There are also no-show passengers. They leave when they were informed to board the plane. It seriously affected the operation of the flight, especially when the passengers leave during the stopover.

Therefore, it is important for passengers to arrive at the airport and complete the formalities in advance, pay attention to the boarding time of the flight, and get on the plane as soon as possible. If you need to change the itinerary, please contact the airport.

Decide whether the following statements are true (T) or false (F) according to the passage

(1) Flight delay means that the arrival time of one flight is less than 15 minutes later than the scheduled arrival time. (   )

(2) The weather reasons contain a lot much more than heavy snow, rain or fog, etc. (   )

(3) The reason for air traffic control is that the military temporarily controls the airspace. (   )

(4) Once the mechanical troubles are found, it means the flight will be cancelled. (   )

(5) Some passengers used to arrive at the airport very late, which caused the flight to be delayed. (   )

Unit 12　Entry Forms and Transfer

Learning Objectives

1. Be familiar with the regulations of the CIQ.
2. Know how to help passengers to transfer.
3. Grasp relevant English words and expressions.
4. Know the cabin attendants' responsibilities.

Part One　Listening

1 Listen to the dialogue and choose the best answer to each question

(1) What's the destination the passenger wants to go?

A. Hong Kong

B. Shanghai

C. Sydney

(2) How long does it leave the passenger to transfer?

A. 20 minutes

B. 16 minutes

C. 30 minutes

2 Listen to the dialogue and fill in the blanks

(A cabin attendant is welcoming passengers on board.)

CA: cabin attendant　　PAX: passenger

CA: Excuse me, madam. Would you please _____(1)_____ before we arrive at Beijing?

PAX: What is this form for?

CA: It's an entry form. You will need it when you _____(2)_____.

PAX: OK. Do I have to fill them on board?

CA: It is suggested, because it will _____(3)_____ going through the CIQ.

PAX: All right. Do I need to return to you when I finish it?

CA: No, madam. You need to _____(4)_____ when you go through the Customs.

听力音频

PAX: Can I ask you for help if I meet some difficulties when filling it?

CA: Sure. _____5_____ .

PAX: Thanks.

CA: You are welcome.

Part Two Dialogues

AC: airport crew   CA: cabin attendant   PAX: passenger

1 Dialogue 1

(Tom has landed at Hong Kong International Airport. He is late for his connecting flight to Tianjin due to the delay. He has to go to the Flight Connections Center to make a new transit.)

PAX: Excuse me, Miss. I missed my connecting flight to Tianjin due to the delay. May I make a new transit?

AC: Certainly, sir. We will make an alternate arrangement for you.

PAX: It's OK. But I hope to get to Tianjin as early as possible for some business reasons.

AC: Let me check it for you ... According to the system, you could take flight CA4592 which leaves Hong Kong at 9:20 a.m.

PAX: Is it a direct flight or a connecting flight?

AC: Connecting flight. You have to transit in Chengdu.

PAX: Can I have direct flights today?

AC: Yes, you can take flight CA4066 which is non-stop to Tianjin. But the departure time is at 14:10. It will arrive at Tianjin Airport at 18:05 this evening.

PAX: Oh, it doesn't matter. I prefer the direct flight. Please book that for me. I'm a little tired after the transfer.

AC: OK. Here you are, sir. I do apologize for any inconvenience caused by the delay.

PAX: It's OK. Do I need to check in now?

AC: No, you don't have to. There are still several hours before check-in. You could go around the airport and have a rest.

PAX: I see. Many thanks.

AC: It's my pleasure.

2 Dialogue 2

(A passenger will transfer midway, so he asks the cabin attendant for help.)

PAX: Excuse me, Miss. It is the midway stop for me and I'll stay here for only about 50 minutes. Should I take all my belongings with me when I deplane here?

CA: It depends. If you are continuing your journey with us, your carry-on baggage could be left on board, but take the valuables and important documents with you. The ground staff will give you a re-boarding ticket when you disembark.

PAX: But I will take another flight.

CA: It means you will transfer to another flight at this airport. Then you need to take all your belongings and check at the transfer counter in the terminal building. They will be very glad to help you.

PAX: How about my checked baggage?

CA: The checked baggage will be claimed at the baggage claim center in the terminal.

PAX: OK. Thank you!

CA: You are welcome.

3 Dialogue 3

(The flight attendant is handing out the entry forms to the passengers on board.)

CA: Excuse me, sir. You are requested to fill in the entry forms before landing.

PAX: Why do I need to fill in the entry form?

CA: It is a necessary document when you pass the CIQ.

PAX: What does CIQ stand for?

CA: It refers to Customs, Immigration and Quarantine.

PAX: Can I write French in this form?

CA: Sorry, sir. Only Chinese and English meet the requirements. If you find it difficult in filling in the forms, I'll be happy to help you.

PAX: Thank you. Do I have to hand it back to you when I finish?

CA: No. Just put it inside your passport and submit them to the officers.

PAX: Are there any other documents needed when I go through the entry formalities?

CA: Yes. You also need to get your passport, visa, health certificate and Customs declaration form ready in advance. That will save your time.

PAX: Thank you. I'll finish it on board.

4 Dialogue 4

(A passenger is puzzled when he fills in the Incoming Passenger Card of Australia. He asks a cabin attendant for help.)

PAX: Excuse me, Miss. I meet some difficulties when filling in the card. Would you please explain it to me?

CA: Sure. Go ahead, please.

PAX: I have brought two bottles of liquor and 200 cigarettes to my friend as gifts. Do I have to pay duty for them?

CA: What is the volume of each bottle of liquor?

PAX: It's 500 mL for each bottle.

CA: I think the Customs officials will let them pass, because they don't exceed the duty-free limits. If you are not sure about anything else, please refer to the Customs Declaration Regulations for the items required for declaration.

PAX: OK. Should I list all the dutiable items, including my personal property?

CA: You'd better do it. All the dutiable items which are not listed on the Declaration Form will be subject to heavy fines.

PAX: Do I need to answer all the questions listed on the card?

CA: Yes, and don't forget to sign your name and the date for declaration on the bottom of this card.

PAX: I won't. Thank you very much.

CA: You are welcome.

5 Words and expressions

Flight Connections Center 航班中转中心
alternate B[ɔːlˈtɜːnət]/A[ˈɔːltərnət] adj. 交替的；轮流的
direct flight 直达班机
non-stop B[ˌnɒn ˈstɒp]/A[ˌnɒn ˈstɒp] adj. 直达的；不在途中停留的
midway [ˌmɪdˈweɪ] adv. 在中途；在两地之间
deplane [diːˈpleɪn] v. 下飞机
disembark B[ˌdɪsɪmˈbɑːk]/A[ˌdɪsɪmˈbɑːrk] v. 下（车、船、飞机等）
transfer counter 转机柜台
terminal building 航站楼
claim [kleɪm] v. 索取；认领 n. 声明；索赔
baggage claim center 行李认领处；行李索取处
entry form 入境表格
Customs [ˈkʌstəmz] n. 海关
Immigration [ˌɪmɪˈɡreɪʃn] n. 移民局检查站
Quarantine [ˈkwɒrəntiːn] n. 检疫部门
passport B[ˈpɑːspɔːt]/A[ˈpæspɔːrt] n. 护照
entry formality 入境手续
health certificate 健康证明
visa [ˈviːzə] n. 签证
declaration [ˌdekləˈreɪʃn] n. 申报（单）；公告；宣言
liquor B[ˈlɪkə(r)]/A[ˈlɪkər] n. 烈性酒；含酒精饮料
volume B[ˈvɒljuːm]/A[ˈvɑːljəm] n. 体积；容积
fine [faɪn] n. 罚金；罚款

6 Notes to the dialogues

(1) It is a necessary document when you pass the CIQ.
这是通过一关两检的必要文件。

(2) ...they don't exceed the duty-free limits.

……他们没有超过免税限额。

(3) ...please refer to the Customs Declaration Regulations for the items required for declaration.

……关于海关需要申报的物品,请参阅海关报关的有关条例。

Part Three Announcements

1 Transfer announcement

Ladies and gentlemen,

We have just landed at _____ airport. It is _____ (a.m./p.m.) local time. The temperature outside is _____ degrees Celsius (_____ Fahrenheit.) Please remain seated until our aircraft stops completely. Please be careful when retrieving items from the overhead compartment.

Passengers leaving the aircraft at this airport, please take your passport and all your belongings to complete the entry formalities in the terminal. Your checked baggage may be claimed in the baggage claim area.

Passengers continuing to _____ , attention please! The aircraft will stay here for about _____ hour(s). When you disembark, please get your transit card from the ground staff, and complete your entry formalities and quarantine here.

According to Customs regulations of the PRC, please take all carry-on items with you when you go through the Customs. Any baggage left on board will be handed by the Customs. Formalities for checked baggage will be completed at _____ .

Your crew will be changing here. Thank you for flying with us. Have a pleasant day!

2 Announcement for entry forms

Ladies and gentlemen,

Now we are very happy to provide you with entry forms. It is advised to complete them on board to save your time going through Customs, Immigration and Quarantine. If you have any questions while filling in the forms, please don't hesitate to call us for help. We will be happy to help you. When you go through the entry formalities, please submit the completed forms to officials.

Thank you!

3 Announcement for China quarantine regulations

Ladies and gentlemen,

May I have your attention please? In order to protect your and others' health on board, according to the quarantine regulations of China, if you have any symptoms such as fever, chills, weak, vomiting, diarrhea, rash, or you come from some specific African countries, or you have ever been to those countries in 21 days, please contact our crew as soon as possible, or any other questions you could consult the Quarantine official later. Quarantine officials may carry out health quarantine on your arrival.

Thank you for your cooperation!

 Announcement for Australian entry quarantine

Ladies and gentlemen,

Australia has strict security laws that affect you. You will receive an Incoming Passenger Card that asks questions about what you are bringing to Australia and the places you have visited. You must answer these questions truthfully. Any false statement may result in a penalty. It will be checked by officials on your arrival.

You must mark "yes" on your card if you have certain food, plant or animal products, or equipment or shoes used in rivers and lakes or with soil attached. Food supplied on board must be left on board.

If you are not feeling well, particularly with fever, chills or sweats, it is important for your own health and for the others that you bring this to the attention of a member of the crew.

Thank you!

 Announcement for declaration

Ladies and gentlemen,

Attention, please. All passengers have to declare all the items dutiable in your baggage. You may see the notices at the airport, which tell you what you need to declare. Or you could refer to the Customs declaration form for details. It is important because any false declaration would result in fines or penalty on the spot.

Thank you!

 Words and phrases

Celsius ['selsiəs] *adj.* 摄氏的
Fahrenheit ['færənhaɪt] *adj.* 华氏的
retrieve [rɪ'tri:v] *v.* 取回
symptom ['sɪmptəm] *n.* 症状；征候
chills [tʃɪlz] *n.* 着凉；伤寒
diarrhea [ˌdaɪə'rɪə] *n.* 腹泻
rash [ræʃ] *n.* 皮疹
consult [kən'sʌlt] *v.* 咨询；请教
penalty ['penəlti] *n.* 惩罚；处罚

declare B[dɪˈkleə(r)]/A[dɪˈkler] v. 公布;宣告;申报

on the spot 在现场;立即;当场

Part Four　Role Play

In small groups, make up a dialogue based on the following situations

(1) A passenger will transfer when the flight lands midway at Beijing Airport. The cabin attendant comes to help him with what he needs to do.

(2) A passenger meets some difficulties when filling in the entry forms. The cabin attendant is required to solve his problem.

Part Five　Exercise

1　Fill in the blanks in the following dialogues

Dialogue 1

PAX: Excuse me, Miss. I missed my connecting flight due to the delay. Could you make a new transit for me?

CA: Certainly, sir. ＿＿＿＿＿(1)＿＿＿＿＿（我们会为您做一个航班备选安排）.

PAX: It's OK. But I hope to get to Beijing as early as possible.

CA: Let me see ... You could take flight CA1032 ＿＿＿＿＿(2)＿＿＿＿＿（将于上午10点起飞）.

PAX: Is it a direct flight or connecting flight?

CA: Connecting flight. ＿＿＿＿＿(3)＿＿＿＿＿（您需要在南京中转）.

PAX: Do you have direct flights today?

CA: Yes, ＿＿＿＿＿(4)＿＿＿＿＿（您可以搭乘直飞北京的CA2208次航班）. But the departure time is at 12:10. It will be a little late.

PAX: It doesn't matter. I prefer the direct flight. Please book that for me.

CA: OK. Here you are, sir. ＿＿＿＿＿(5)＿＿＿＿＿（由于延误给您带来的不便,我们深表歉意）.

PAX: Many thanks.

CA: It's my pleasure.

Dialogue 2

CA: Excuse me, sir. ＿＿＿＿＿(6)＿＿＿＿＿（您需要填写一下这张入境表）before landing.

PAX: Why do I need to fill in it?

CA: It is a necessary document when you pass the CIQ.

PAX: What does CIQ stand for?

CA：It refers to _____(7)_____ （海关、移民局检查站和检疫检查站）.

PAX：Can I write Japanese in this form?

CA：Sorry, sir. Only Chinese and English meet the requirements. _____(8)_____ （如果您在填表时遇到困难，我非常乐意提供帮助）.

PAX：Thank you. Do I have to hand it back to you when I finish?

CA：No. _____(9)_____ （把表夹在护照中即可）.

PAX：Are there any other documents needed?

CA：Yes. You need to get your passport, visa, health certificate ready. _____(10)_____ （这会节省您的时间）.

PAX：Thank you.

CA：It's my pleasure.

2 Translate the following phrases into English

(1) 直航　　　　　　　　(2) 直飞

(3) 下飞机　　　　　　　(4) 中转

(5) 索取　　　　　　　　(6) 入境表

(7) 海关　　　　　　　　(8) 移民局检查站

(9) 检疫检查站　　　　　(10) 护照

(11) 入境手续　　　　　 (12) 签证

(13) 申报　　　　　　　 (14) 罚款

3 Translate the following sentences into English

(1) 您的随身行李可以留在机上，但请随身携带贵重物品和重要证件。

(2) 您需要带走所有行李，并在航站楼的转机柜台查询。

(3) 如果您不确定其他事项，请参阅海关申报条例。

(4) 所有未在申报表中列出的应缴税品将被处以高额罚款。

(5) 不要忘记在卡片底部签上您的姓名和日期。

4 Translate the following sentences into Chinese

(1) Is it a direct flight or a connecting flight?

(2) The ground staff will give you a re-boarding ticket when you disembark.

(3) The checked baggage will be claimed at the baggage claim center in the terminal.

(4) It is a necessary document when you pass the CIQ.

(5) I think the Customs officials will let them pass.

5 Fill in the entry form

■ Incoming Passenger Card • Australia		YOU MUST ANSWER EVERY QUESTION - IF UNSURE, ☒ YES.		
◆Family Name		◆Are you bringing into Australia:		
◆Given Name		1. Goods that may be prohibited, such as medicines, weapons of any kind or illicit drugs?	Yes ☐	No ☐
◆Passport Number		2. More than 1125ml of alcohole or 250 cigarettes or 250g of tobacco products?	Yes ☐	No ☐
◆Flight Number		3. Goods abtained overseas with a combined total price of more than AUD$400?	Yes ☐	No ☐
◆Intended Address in Australia		4. Goods or samples for business/commercial use?	Yes ☐	No ☐
		5. AUD$10,000 or more in Australian or foreign currency equivalent?	Yes ☐	No ☐
	State	6. Any food - includes dried, fresh, preverved, cooked, uncooked?	Yes ☐	No ☐
◆Do you intend to live in Australia for the next 12 months?	Yes ☐ No ☐	7. Wooden articles, plants, traditional medicine/herbs, seeds, bulbs, straw, nuts?	Yes ☐	No ☐
		8. Animals, animal products, eggs, birds, fish, insects, shells, bee products, pets food?	Yes ☐	No ☐
◆If you are not an Australian citizen:		9. Soil, or articles with soil attached?	Yes ☐	No ☐
Do you suffer from Tuberculosis?	Yes ☐ No ☐	10. Have you visited a rural area or farm animals outside Australia in the past 30 days?	Yes ☐	No ☐
Do you have any criminal convictions?	Yes ☐ No ☐	11. Have you been in Africa or South America in the last 6 days?	Yes ☐	No ☐

DECLARATION
The information I have given is true, correct and complete. I understand failure to answer any questions may have serious consequences.

YOUR SIGNATURE DAY MONTH YEAR TURN OVER THE CARD

PLEASE COMPLETE IN ENGLISH	▶ PLEASE ☒ AND ANSWER A OR B OR C					
▶ In which country did you board this flight or ship?	**A** Migrating permanently to Australia ☐	**B** Visitor or temporary entrant ☐				**C** Resident returning to Australia ☐
			Years	Months	Days	
◆ What is your usual occupation?		▶ Your intended length of stay in Australia		OR		▶ Country where you spent most time abroad
▶ Nationality as shown on passport		▶ Your country of residence				
		▶ Your main reason for coming to Australia (☒ one only)				
▶ Date of birth Day Month Year		Convention/conference ☐1 Employment ☐4 Holiday ☐7				MAKE SURE YOU HAVE COMPLETED BOTH SIDES OF THIS CARD.
		Business ☐2 Education ☐5 Other ☐8				PRESENT THIS CARD ON ARRIVAL WITH YOUR PASSPORT.
		Visiting friends of relatives ☐3 Exhibition ☐6				

Information sought on this form is required to administer immigration, customs, quarantine, statistical, health, wildlife and currency laws of Australia and its collection is authorised by legislation. It will be disclosed only to agencies administering these areas and those entitled to receive it under Australian law. the leaflet Safeguarding your personal

Commonwealth of Australia 2002
15 (Design date 07/02)
McMILLAN PRINT

Part Six Supplementary Reading

Australian Quarantine and Customs Regulations

When you travel, each country has its own immigration and border protection requirements. The Australian Department of Immigration and Border Protection manages the movement of goods and people across the Australian border, while each state and territory enforces their own local quarantine restrictions.

There are a few items that we come across, or get asked about often. Some of them are allowed, some are not, and some require a permit before bringing them in. Even if an item is allowed, there might be some caveats. Here are some of the common ones.

Food

Food items brought to Australia need to be declared on your Incoming Passenger Card if you come by plane, or on the parcels you mail. Australia has very strict biosecurity procedures at our international borders to prevent the introduction of harmful pests and diseases. Certain food items brought to Australia, even small amounts or ingredients for cooking, need to be declared.

Generally, most biscuits, bread, cakes, chocolate, tea, coffee and seed oil for personal consumption are allowed to bring to Australia. Other food items, for example, cheese, butter, dairy products, dried herbs, fish, soft drink, noodles, and meat must be declared and inspected on arrival. Products that do not meet import conditions will be exported or destroyed at the importer's expense.

Duty-free Goods

Duty-free goods bought overseas could be brought to Australia. But remember: don't go over your duty-free limits, for example, alcohol no more than 2.25 liters, tobacco no more than 25 cigarettes or 25g tobacco. Families coming back to Australia on the same flight or voyage may combine their individual duty-free concession limits. To do this, families must stay together when going through Customs clearance. For example, a family of two adults and two children would have a combined duty-free allowance of AUD 2700. If in doubt, always declare. Penalties may apply if goods are not declared. If you bring in more than your duty-free allowance for general goods, you'll need to pay duty on all your general goods not just on the excess.

Powders & Liquids

Powders are fine dry particles produced by the grinding, crushing, or disintegration of a solid substance, for example flour, sugar, ground coffee, spices, powdered milk, baby formula or cosmetics. An inorganic powder is a powder not consisting of, or derived from, any living matter. There is no limit on organic powders, such as food and powdered baby formula. The total volume of inorganic powders must not exceed 350 milliliters or 350 grams per person.

A liquid is a substance that is liquid at room temperature. All liquids must be in containers of 100 milliliters or 100 grams or less. Containers must fit into one transparent and re-sealable plastic bag, like a snap-lock bag. The four sides of the bag's sealed area must add up to no more than 80 centimeters (e.g. 20 cm× 20cm or 15 cm×25cm).

When arriving in Australia, you'll need to present your passport and Incoming Passenger Card. After collecting your baggage, if you have nothing to declare, you proceed through the green channel. If you have something to declare, proceed through the red channel. Random baggage inspections are standard procedures at all international airports.

Decide whether the following statements are true (T) or false (F) according to the passage

(1) Bread, cakes, tea, coffee for personal consumption are allowed to bring to Australia. (   )

(2) Dairy products, fish, soft drinks and meat can be brought to Australia without declaration. (   )

(3) One bottle of liquor with volume under 1 liter can be brought to Australia duty free. (   )

(4) Families coming back to Australia on the same flight cannot combine their individual duty-free concession limits. (   )

(5) There is no limit on powdered baby formula. (   )

Module 4　Emergency Situation

Unit 13　First Aid

Learning Objectives

1. Be familiar with various special situations.
2. Know how to serve sick passengers.
3. Know how to give announcements when passengers are sick in flight.
4. Grasp relevant English expressions.

Part One　Listening

1 Listen to the dialogue and choose the best answer to each question

(1) What's wrong with the passenger's son?
A. He cannot speak.
B. He cannot breathe.
C. He chokes on a piece of food.

(2) How does the cabin attendant help?
A. She asks the boy to cough.
B. She lays the boy across her lap.
C. All the above.

2 Listen to the dialogue and fill in the blanks

(A passenger presses the call button and the cabin attendant comes over.)
CA: cabin attendant　PAX: passenger
CA: Excuse me, sir. ＿＿＿＿(1)＿＿＿＿? What can I do for you?
PAX: Yes, Miss. I feel awful here.
CA: How long ＿＿＿＿(2)＿＿＿＿?

听力音频

PAX: It is about half an hour after boarding. I feel drumming in my ear, and I also feel sick.

CA: Have you ever suffered from _____(3)_____ before?

PAX: No, this is my first time to _____(4)_____.

CA: Don't worry, you've probably been airsick. I will get some medicine for you.

PAX: Thank you very much.

CA: Here is the medicine. After taking this, you can close your eyes and have a nap. By the way, an airsickness bag can be found in your seat pocket. _____(5)_____, you can use it.

Part Two Dialogue

1 Dialogue 1

CA: Did you press the call button, sir? What's the matter?

PAX: I have pain in my stomach and back, and I feel very cold.

CA: I'm sorry to hear that, sir. Is there anything I can do for you?

PAX: Could you give me something hot to drink?

CA: What would you like, tea or coffee?

PAX: Just give me a cup of hot water, please.

CA: Wait for a moment, I will be right back.

CA: Here you are, sir. It's hot, mind your hand. We have some medicine for stomachache. I have brought it for you.

PAX: That's very kind of you.

(20 minutes later.)

CA: Do you feel better?

PAX: Even worse. I feel like vomiting.

CA: Don't worry. I will page for a doctor.

(Announcement)

Ladies and gentlemen, may I have your attention, please? There is a sick passenger on board. If there is a doctor or a nurse on this flight, please contact us immediately. Thank you!

(a few minutes later.)

CA: I'm sorry to tell you there is no doctor or nurse on board. But we have informed the ground staff and they will take you to the hospital as soon as we reach the airport.

PAX: Thank you a thousand times.

CA: Don't mention it. This is my duty!

2 Dialogue 2

CA: Did you press the call button, madam? What's the matter?

PAX: I'm feeling sick. The earache is killing me.

CA: Oh, I'm sorry to hear that. That was due to a change in air pressure. You can relieve it by swallowing or chewing gums.

PAX: I know. I've chewed gums since take-off, but it didn't work at all.

CA: Let me get you some water. Hold your breath and swallow at the same time.

PAX: Thank you. I'll try.

(After taking some water.)

CA: Does it help?

PAX: No.

CA: Let me tell you another way to deal with it. Firstly, you take a deep breath, then try to stop your nose with your fingers and blow your nose. Like this. (The CA shows her how to do that.)

PAX: It works now. Thank you very much. Oh, my baby looks agitated. I think he has the same problem. Can you help me mix this milk powder with warm water, please?

CA: Where is her bottle?

PAX: In my bag under my seat. Could you get it for me, please?

CA: No problem. What else do you need?

PAX: A spare diaper please.

CA: OK. I'll be back in a minute.

(One minute later.)

CA: Here they are... milk and nappy. Hope she'll be fine.

PAX: Thanks. You are so kind.

CA: You're welcome.

3 Dialogue 3

CA: Excuse me, madam. What would you like to drink? We have coffee, water and tea.

PAX: No, thanks. Please give me medication for airsickness. I'm not feeling well.

CA: OK, I'll get something for you right away. Here is some motion sickness medication and a cup of hot water.

PAX: Thank you very much. You are really helpful.

CA: It's my pleasure. You'd better take medication and sit for a while. You'll be feeling better soon.

PAX: OK. But could you give me an airsickness bag? I'm afraid I might be sick.

CA: You can find it in the pocket of the seat in front of you.

PAX: Oh, yes, here it is.

CA: If you still need any more help, please don't hesitate to ask us.

PAX: Fine. Thank you again.

4 Dialogue 4

(A little boy is crying.)

CA: What happened to your son, madam?

PAX1: He was running about in the cabin and knocked his head against the seat.

CA: Let me see. Oh, he's got a bump on his head and it's bruised.

PAX1: Does he need to take some aspirin?

CA: I don't think so. It's not serious. I'll get you a pack. (To the boy.) A little bit painful?

BOY: Yeah. And my arm, it hurts too.

CA: Please sit down and let me check. Oh dear, it seems that it might be broken. I'll page for a doctor.

(Announcement)

Ladies and gentlemen, may I have your attention, please? There is a passenger who broke his arm. If there is a doctor or a nurse on this flight, please make yourself known to a member of the crew immediately by pressing your call bell. Thank you.

PAX2: Excuse me. I'm a doctor. What's the problem?

CA: The little boy broke his arm.

PAX2: Do you have a bandage?

CA: Yes. Here you are.

PAX2: I'll put your arm into a sling. (The doctor places the boy's arm into a sling.)

BOY: Thank you.

CA: Here is your medicine. Don't worry. You'll be all right. I'll come back to check in a few minutes.

5 Dialogue 5

(A passenger is suffering from indigestion.)

CA: Did you call us, sir? What can I do for you?

PAX1: Oh. I have a pain in my stomach.

CA: What kind of pain, sir?

PAX1: A pain in the middle of my stomach.

CA: Have you had this pain before?

PAX1: No, I don't think so.

CA: Is the pain anywhere else, sir? I mean if you have a pain in your arms, or your back.

PAX1: No, no ... Just here in the middle.

CA: Are your fingers tingling?

PAX1: Not really.

CA: Have you eaten something in a hurry?

PAX1: Hmm yes. I just had some spicy food before I boarded the plane.

CA: OK, sir. I think you are suffering from indigestion. Shall I bring you some medicine?

PAX1：Sure.

　　　(A passenger's nose is bleeding.)

PAX2：Excuse me, could you give me some napkins? My nose has continued bleeding for 2 minutes.

CA：Madam, please lean your head a little bit forward and pinch your nose with your thumb and your forefinger like this.

PAX2：How long do I need to pinch my nose like this?

CA：At least 10 minutes. Please do not raise your head, otherwise, the blood will run into your throat. It's very dangerous.

PAX2：I'll try … Yes, it works. Thank you.

6 Words and expressions

stomach ['stʌmək] n. 胃；腹部

stomachache ['stʌməkeɪk] n. 胃痛；腹痛

medicine B ['medsn]/A ['medɪsn] n. 药

vomit B ['vɒmɪt]/A ['vɑːmɪt] v. 呕吐；吐

earache B ['ɪəreɪk]/A ['ɪreɪk] n. 耳痛

swallow B ['swɒləʊ]/A ['swɑːloʊ] v. 吞下；咽下；（由于紧张等）做吞咽动作 n. 吞；咽；一次吞咽的量；一口

chew [tʃuː] v. 咀嚼；嚼碎 n. 咀嚼

breath [breθ] n. 吸气

blow B [bləʊ]/A [bloʊ] v. 吹；刮；（被）刮动；吹动

agitated ['ædʒɪteɪtɪd] adj. 焦虑不安的；激动的

milk powder 奶粉

diaper B ['daɪpə(r)]/A ['daɪpər] n. 尿片；（婴儿的）尿布

medication B [ˌmedɪ'keɪʃn]/A [ˌmedɪ'keɪʃn] n. 药；药物

hesitate ['hezɪteɪt] v.（对某事）犹豫；迟疑不决；顾虑；疑虑

run about 乱跑

bump [bʌmp] n. 肿块；撞击；隆起 v. 碰撞；颠簸而行

bruised B [bruːzd]/A [bruzd] v. 挫伤；（使）出现伤痕

aspirin B ['æsprɪn]/A ['æsperɪn] n.（药）阿司匹林（具有解热镇痛的作用）

cold pack 冰袋

painful ['peɪnfl] adj. 痛苦的；疼痛的

page [peɪdʒ] v. 呼叫 n. 页；面

call bell 呼叫铃，同 call button

bandage ['bændɪdʒ] n. 绷带 v. 用绷带包扎

sling [slɪŋ] n. 悬带；吊索 v. 吊起；悬挂

indigestion [ˌɪndɪ'dʒestʃən] n. 消化不良（症）

tingling ['tɪŋglɪŋ] n. 刺痛感

lean [liːn] v.倾斜;倚 adj.瘦且健康的;贫乏的;无脂肪的 n.瘦肉

pinch [pɪntʃ] v.掐;夹痛;使入不敷出 n.捏;少量;一撮

thumb [θʌm] n.拇指

forefinger B[ˈfɔːfɪŋɡə(r)]/A[ˈfɔːrfɪŋɡə(r)] n.食指

7 Notes to the dialogues

(1) I'm sorry to hear that.

听到这个消息我很抱歉。(这句话常用于听到别人说不好的事情表达同情。)

(2) We have some medicine for stomachache.

我们有治胃疼的药。

(3) I will page for a doctor.

我来广播找医生。page for 表示"(通过扩音器、广播等)呼叫"。

(4) You can relieve it by swallowing and chewing gums.

您可以通过吞咽动作和嚼口香糖来缓解这一症状。chewing gums 在句中作动名词，表示"嚼口香糖"，也可以用作名词，表示"口香糖"。

(5) Please give me medication for airsickness.

请给我拿一些晕机药。

(6) Here is some motion sickness medication and a cup of hot water.

这是晕机药和热水。motion sickness medication 晕车药、晕机药。

(7) He was running about in the cabin and knocked his head against the seat.

他在客舱里乱跑,把头撞到椅子上了。knock against 表示"撞到"。

(8) Please lean your head a little bit forward and pinch your nose with your thumb and your forefinger like this.

请稍微前倾头部,用大拇指和食指捏住鼻子。

Part Three Announcements

1 Medical situation

Ladies and gentlemen,

May I have your attention, please? There is a sick passenger on board. If there is a doctor or a nurse on this flight, please contact the cabin attendant immediately.

Thank you.

广播音频

2 Medical problem

Ladies and gentlemen,

This is the captain speaking. Because of mechanical problems that need correction, we have decided to make an additional stop and land at _____ airport at _____ a.m./p.m. If there is further information, we will inform you as soon as possible. We apologize for the inconvenience caused.

Thank you for your cooperation.

3 Diversion for sick passengers

Ladies and gentlemen,

May I have your attention, please? We have a sick passenger in need of urgent medical treatment. The captain has decided to land immediately at Nanjing Lukou Airport. We expect to arrive there in approximately 20 minutes.

Thank you for your understanding and support!

4 Landing with sick passengers

Ladies and gentlemen,

We have a very sick passenger who needs urgent medical treatment. Please remain in your seat and keep the aisle clear, so that medical personnels can provide on-board medical rescue as soon as possible/ so that the sick passenger can disembark as soon as possible for further treatment.

Thank you for your understanding and support!

5 Word and phrase

urgent B['ɜːdʒnet]/A['ɜːrdʒənt] *adj.* 紧急的；急迫的；极力主张的
approximately B[ə'prɒksɪmətli]/A[ə'prɑːksɪmətli] *adv.* 大约；近似地
treatment ['triːtmənt] *n.* 治疗；对待
rescue ['reskjuː] *n.* 救援；营救
medical personnel 医务人员
medical treatment 医疗救治

6 Notes to the announcement

(1) We apologize for the inconvenience caused.
给您带来不便我们深表歉意。

(2) Please remain in your seat and keep the aisle clear, so that medical personnels can provide on-board medical rescue as soon as possible/ so that the sick passenger can disembark as soon as possible for further treatment.
请坐好并保持过道畅通，以便医务人员尽快实施机上医疗救助/以便生病的旅客可以尽快下飞机进行下一步治疗。

Part Four Role Play

In small groups, make up a dialogue based on the following situations

(1) A passenger on board requires immediate medical treatment. As there is no doctor on board, the captain decides to make an emergency landing. Tell the passenger you have everything ready.

(2) A passenger has a stomachache and feels like vomiting. Help him to lie down and find a nurse on board to take care of him.

Part Five Exercises

1 Fill in the blanks in the following dialogues

Dialogue 1

CA: Excuse me, sir. Did you press the call button? What can I do for you?

PAX: Yes, I _____(1)_____ (感到恶心). I don't know what is going on.

CA: Have you ever suffered from _____(2)_____ (晕机)?

PAX: No, this is my first time taking a flight. I just have _____(3)_____ (耳鸣).

CA: You just need to _____(4)_____ (咀嚼) some gums. It will be better soon.

PAX: It doesn't work at all. I have already had two pieces of _____(5)_____ (口香糖).

CA: Then I will give you a cup of water. _____(6)_____ (屏住呼吸) and swallow at the same time.

PAX: Thank you. I'll try.

CA: _____(7)_____ (您现在感觉怎么样)?

PAX: Yes, I feel better now. Thanks for your help.

CA: Please don't mention it. It's my duty.

Dialogue 2

CA: What's going on, madam?

PAX: I've got _____(8)_____ (头疼). I feel _____(9)_____ (冷) in both my hands and feet.

CA: I'm sorry to hear that. What can I do for you?

PAX: Could you please give me a cup of hot water?

CA: OK. I will also give you some medicine.

PAX: Thank you, you are so thoughtful.

CA: How do you feel now?

PAX: Even worse. I _____(10)_____ (想吐).

CA: Let me help you go to the _____(11)_____ (前舱). There are _____(12)_____ (空座) there, I can take out the armrest and let you lie down… Here we are. Sit down here. Please lie down. The airsickness bag is in your seat pocket. If you feel sick, you may use it. Is it any better now?

PAX: Thank you. I feel a lot better.

2 Translate the following phrases into English

(1) 座椅口袋 (2) 医疗救治

(3) 医务人员 (4) 晕机

（5）奶粉　　　　　　　　（6）呕吐

（7）屏住呼吸　　　　　　（8）乱跑

（9）消化不良(症)　　　　 （10）擤鼻子

3 Translate the following sentences into English

（1）我想您可能是晕机了。我去给您拿点药。

（2）您可以通过吞咽或者嚼口香糖来缓解它。

（3）前舱有些空余座位，我来帮您躺下。

（4）您现在感觉如何？

（5）如果本次航班上有医生或者护士，请立即与任意一位乘务员联系。

4 Translate the following sentences into Chinese

（1）Excuse me, sir. Did you press the call button?

（2）We have a very sick passenger in need of urgent medical treatment.

（3）Don't worry. I will page for a doctor.

（4）The captain has informed the ground staff and you'll be sent to the hospital once our plane arrives at the airport.

（5）We have some medicine for indigestion.

5 Match the words or expressions with proper definition

(1) first aid kit　　　　A. It stops bleeding and protects small wounds.

(2) airsickness bag　　 B. To bring food or drink up from your stomach out through your mouth. Because you are ill.

(3) nose drop　　　　　C. A medical condition in which you have a very high temperature.

(4) bandage　　　　　　D. A special liquid which you put into your nose to relieve stuffiness.

(5) dizzy　　　　　　　E. Feeling unable to stand steadily.

(6) fever　　　　　　　F. An area of skin that is bruised because you have hit it on something.

(7) bump　　　　　　　G. A special box contains medicines and items to treat people who are injured.

(8) vomit　　　　　　　H. A plastic waste bag for vomiting.

Part Six　Supplementary Reading

First Aid

First aid — the care given before emergency medical help arrives — can literally mean the difference between life and death. But knowing the correct thing to do if someone has a nosebleed or cut is also important.

Choking

Choking occurs when a foreign object lodges in the throat or windpipe, blocking the flow of air. In adults, a piece of food is often the culprit. Young children often swallow small objects. Because choking cuts off oxygen to the brain, must give first aid as quickly as possible. Heimlich maneuver is an emergency rescue procedure for application to someone choking on a foreign object.

Stand behind the person. Place one foot slightly in front of the other for balance. Wrap your arms around the waist. Tip the person forward slightly. If a child is choking, kneel down behind the child.

Make a fist with one hand. Position it slightly above the person's navel.

Grasp the fist with the other hand. Press hard into the abdomen with a quick, upward thrust — as if trying to lift the person up.

Perform between 6 and 10 abdominal thrusts. Until the blockage is dislodged.

Fainting

Fainting occurs when your brain temporarily doesn't receive enough blood supply, causing you to lose consciousness. This loss of consciousness is usually brief. If a passenger faints:

Position the person on his or her back. If there are no injuries and the person is breathing, raise the person's legs above heart level — about 12 inches (30 centimeters) — if possible. Loosen belts, collars or other constrictive clothing.

To reduce the chance of fainting again, don't get the person up too quickly. If the person doesn't regain consciousness within one minute, call 120 or your local emergency number.

Check for breathing. If the person isn't breathing, begin CPR. Call 120 or your local emergency number. Continue CPR until help arrives or the person begins to breathe. If the person was injured in a fall associated with a faint, treat bumps, bruises or cuts appropriately, control bleeding with direct pressure.

Nosebleeds

Nosebleeds are common. Most often they are a nuisance and not a true medical problem. But they can be both.

Sit upright and lean forward. By remaining upright, you reduce blood pressure in the veins of your nose. This discourages further bleeding. Sitting forward will help you avoid swallowing blood, which can irritate your stomach.

Gently blow your nose. Blow your nose to clear your nose of blood clots. Then spray both sides of your nose with a nasal decongestant containing oxymetazoline (Afrin).

Pinch your nose. Use your thumb and index finger to pinch your nostrils shut. Breathe through your mouth. Continue to pinch for 10 to 15 minutes. Pinching sends pressure to the bleeding point on the nasal septum and often stops the flow of blood.

If the bleeding continues after 10 to 15 minutes, repeat holding pressure for another 10 to 15 minutes. Avoid peeking at your nose. If the bleeding still continues, seek emergency care.

To prevent re-bleeding, don't pick or blow your nose and don't bend down for several hours. Keep your head higher than the level of your heart. You can also gently apply some petroleum jelly to the inside of your nose using a cotton swab or your finger.

If re-bleeding occurs, go through these steps again. Call the doctor if the bleeding continues.

Decide whether the following statements are true (T) or false (F) according to the passage

(1) After the person regains his consciousness, flight attendants first should help him stand up so that he can feel his way around and hence reduce the chance of fainting again. (   )

(2) There are different approaches in terms of doing the Heimlich maneuver to people from different age groups. (   )

(3) When fainting occurs, you should first start by giving breath if they become unconscious and then begin performing CPR. (   )

(4) The correct way of doing Heimlich maneuver is making a fist with one hand and grasping with the other and make sure your arms are round the person's chest before the upward abdominal thrusts. (   )

(5) If a passenger faints on the flight, remember do not move him suddenly at first, let him rest a while in his seat in order to see if he can recover by himself. (   )

Unit 14   Emergency Procedures

Learning Objectives

1. Be familiar with various emergency situations.
2. Know how to serve passengers when emergency situations happened.
3. Know how to give announcements when facing emergency situations.
4. Grasp relevant English expressions.

Part One Listening

1 Listen to the dialogue and choose the best answer to each question

(1) Why did the passenger press the call button?

A. She doesn't know how to use the oxygen mask.

B. She can't find the life vest for her baby.

C. She can't find the life vest for herself.

(2) What did the passenger ask for help while she puts her life vest on?

A. Hold her baby

B. Hold her baggage

C. Hold the baby's life vest

2 listen to the following dialogue and fill in the blanks

CA: Ladies and gentlemen, we are entering an area of turbulence. Please ＿＿＿(1)＿＿ ＿＿＿＿ your seat belts. (To a passenger walking in the cabin.) Sir, please return to your seat.

PAX1: But I'd like to go to the ＿＿＿(2)＿＿＿.

CA: Sorry, the lavatories have been closed during the ＿＿＿(3)＿＿＿.

PAX1: Oh, I see.

PAX2: Excuse me, Miss. Could you please show me how to use the ＿＿＿(4)＿＿＿ please?

CA: OK, Look, just pull the mask towards you, then hold it over your nose and mouth and ＿＿＿(5)＿＿＿ normally. Are you clear?

PAX2: I think so. Thank you.

Part Two Dialogues

1 Dialogue 1

PAX: Excuse me, could you tell me how I inflate my life vest?

CA: I suppose you didn't notice the life vest demonstration just now, sir.

PAX: Sorry, I didn't.

CA: Never mind. You can inflate it by pulling these tabs down or you can blow into the mouthpiece. Please remember: don't inflate it in the cabin.

PAX: Could you tell me the reason why we are not suggested inflating the life vest in the cabin.

CA: Let me explain it to you, sir. If all passengers inflate their life vest, there will be no room inside the cabin. Also, some broken metal from the aircraft may damage the life vest on the way out.

PAX: OK. I see. Thank you.

CA: You are welcome.

2 Dialogue 2

CA: Ladies and gentlemen, there are eight emergency exits. Please locate the nearest to you. After landing, please leave by the exit the nearest to you. Got that?

PAX1: Yes.

(The CA turns to a passenger sitting next to an over-wing exit.)

CA: Excuse me, madam. You are sitting next to an emergency exit.

PAX1: Yes, I am.

CA: In the case of an emergency, can you assist us to open the exit, madam?

PAX1: Hmm. I am not sure. Is the door very heavy?

CA: Not too heavy. But if you would like to sit somewhere else, I can arrange another seat for you.

PAX1: OK. Thank you.

(The CA turns to another passenger.)

CA: Excuse me, sir. Would you mind changing your seat with that passenger who sits next to the emergency exit.

PAX2: Not at all.

CA: Thanks for your cooperation.

3 Dialogue 3

CA: Sir, return your seat back to the upright position and fasten your seat belt please.

PAX1: What happened? Anything wrong with the plane?

CA: Due to a mechanical fault, the pressure in the cabin has reduced. Please pull the oxygen mask over your nose and mouth.

PAX1: Oh dear! Are we in danger?

CA: Keep calm. Everything will be right in a moment. (To PAX2.) Quickly, madam. Pull down the mask!

PAX2: What shall I do?

CA: Place the mask over your face and take a deep breath. Are you clear?

PAX2: I think so. Thank you.

CA: Don't panic. Please follow our instructions.

4 Dialogue 4

(The CA is making an announcement about brace for impact.)

CA: Attention, please. On the command of brace for impact, please cross your arms and rest them on the seat in front of you. Place your head on your arms. When the landing is made, the airplane may bounce several times; hold your position until the aircraft has come to a complete stop. Then follow the instructions of the cabin crew.

CA: Excuse me, sir.

PAX: Yes?

CA: I'm sorry, but you must bend over more and place your head between your knees.

PAX: But I can't. It hurts my stomach. I'm too heavy ... my head won't go that far.

CA: OK, sir. Try holding the back of the seat in front of you and place your head between your arms.

PAX: OK, that's better. Thank you.

5 Dialogue 5

Purser: Ladies and gentlemen, may I have your attention, please? We are about to commence an emergency evacuation. Please leave all carry-on luggage behind on board. Please remain calm and make your way to the emergency exit the nearest to you. The floor lighting will guide you to the exit. Remove all sharp objects from your possession. Thank you.

CA: Release your seat belt and get out now.

PAX1: Help! I can't release my seat belt.

CA: Lift up the top of the buckles. Like this.

PAX1: Thanks. I release it now.

PAX2: Excuse me, Miss. Can you get my bag from the overhead locker please?

CA: Leave your bags behind. Quickly now. This way, please.

PAX2: Oh, OK.

PAX3: I can't breathe. Help me ... (*coughs*) The smoke!

CA: Now everyone kneels down on the floor and follows the emergency floor lighting. It will guide you to the exit.

PAX3: But I can't see anything.

CA: Hold onto the person in front of you, and go to the exit.

PAX4: My glasses ... I need my glasses.

CA: Please remove your glasses and your high heel shoes.

PAX4: Why?

CA: It is dangerous when using the emergency escape chute.

PAX4: Well, OK.

(At the exit.)

CA: Now, jump ... jump ... go ... go ... go ... you two stay at the bottom! Help people off!

PAX5: Oh, my God, what is it?

CA: It's an escape slide to get to the ground. Jump and slide down!

PAX5: But I'm terrified of jumping.

CA: Don't be scared. Follow my instructions. Slide off the back of the wing!

6 Words and expressions

inflate [ɪnˈfleɪt] v. 膨胀；使充气
life vest 救生衣
demonstration [ˌdemənˈstreɪʃn] n. 示范；演示
tab [tæb] n. 拉环；小标签
mouthpiece [ˈmaʊθpiːs] n. (乐器的)吹口
pull down 向下拉
metal [ˈmetl] n. 金属
over-wing exit 机翼上方紧急出口
damage [ˈdæmɪdʒ] v. 损害；毁坏
mechanical [məˈkænɪkl] adj. 机械的
fault [fɔːlt] n. 故障
reduce B[rɪˈdjuːs]/A[rɪˈduːs] v. 减少；缩小
oxygen B[ˈɒksɪdʒən]/A[ˈɑːksɪdʒən] n. 氧气
mask B[mɑːsk]/A[mæsk] n. 面罩；面具；面膜
panic [ˈpænɪk] n. 惊恐；恐慌
instruction [ɪnˈstrʌkʃn] n. 指令；教学
emergency landing 紧急降落
failure [ˈfeɪljə(r)] n. 失败；故障
bounce [baʊns] v. 弹起；跳动
bend [bend] v. 弯曲；使弯曲
knee [niː] n. 膝盖
commence [kəˈmens] v. 开始；着手
emergency evacuation 紧急疏散
sharp objects 尖锐物品
possession [pəˈzeʃn] n. (个人)财产；所有物
leave ... behind 把……留下
cough B[kɒf]/A[kɔːf] v. 咳嗽；咳出 n. 咳嗽
kneel [niːl] v. 跪
high heel shoes 高跟鞋
escape chute 紧急疏散软滑梯
bottom B[ˈbɒtəm]/A[ˈbɑːtəm] n. 底部；底面
escape slide 救生滑梯(同 escape chute)
terrified [ˈterɪfaɪd] adj. 恐惧的
scared B[skeəd]/A[skerd] adj. 害怕的；惊慌的

7 Notes to the dialogues

(1) I suppose you didn't notice the life vest demonstration just now, sir.
我猜您刚才没有注意看救生衣的演示。

(2) You can inflate it by pulling these tabs down or you can blow into the mouthpiece.

您可以拉下这两个带子或者用嘴吹气。

(3) Besides, some broken metal from the aircraft may damage your life vest on your way out.

另外,在您出去时,飞机上的金属碎片可能会划破您的救生衣。

(4) Please locate the nearest to you.

请您找到离您最近的(紧急出口)。

(5) After landing, please leave by the exit the nearest to you.

着陆后,请从离您最近的出口撤离。

(6) Our plane will soon make an emergency landing due to the sudden failure of an engine.

由于突发引擎故障,我们的飞机将马上紧急迫降。

(7) Please pull the oxygen mask over your nose and mouth.

请拉下氧气面罩罩住口鼻。

(8) Pull down the mask.

拉下面罩。

(9) Place the mask over your face and take a deep breath.

戴好面罩,深呼吸。

(10) follow instructions

按照指示

(11) brace for impact

指"防冲撞姿势",用于飞机颠簸或水面迫降时减少损伤。

(12) Remove all sharp objects from your possession.

扔掉所有尖锐物品。

Part Three Announcements

Safety demonstration

Ladies and gentlemen,

We will now explain how to use the emergency equipment and where the emergency exits are located.

Your life vest is located under your seat. It can only be used in case of a water landing. Please do not remove it unless instructed by flight attendants.

To put your vest on, simply slip it over your head, then fasten the buckles and pull the straps tightly around your waist.

Upon exiting the aircraft, pull the tabs down firmly to inflate your vest. Please do not inflate your vest while inside the cabin. For further inflation, simply blow into the mouth pieces on either side of your vest. For water landings at night, the sea-light on the

广播音频

vest will be illuminated automatically.

Your oxygen mask is stored above your seat. It will drop down automatically in case of emergency.

When it does so, pull the mask firmly towards you to start the flow of oxygen. Place the mask over your nose and mouth and slip the elastic band over your head. Please put your own mask on before helping others.

When the "Fasten Seat Belt" sign is illuminated, please fasten your seat belt. Simply place the metal tip into the buckle and tighten the strap. To release, just lift up the top of the buckle.

There are 6 emergency exits on this aircraft. They are located in the front, the middle and the rear of the cabin respectively. Please note your nearest exit.

In case of emergency, exit indications and track lighting will illuminate automatically to lead you to the nearest exit.

For additional information, please review the safety instruction card in the seat pocket in front of you.

Thank you!

2 Passenger safety card

Ladies and gentlemen,

May I have your attention, please? You will find a passenger safety card in the rear pocket of the seat in front of you. We strongly advise you to read it before and during the flight. If you have any questions, please don't hesitate to ask one of our cabin attendants. We hope you have an enjoyable flight.

Thank you.

3 Fire in the cabin

Ladies and gentlemen,

We are putting out a minor fire that has broken out in the front cabin. Please remain calm and extinguish all the cigarettes. Passengers sitting in the front, please follow the instructions of our flight attendants. All other passengers, please remain seated and do not walk around in the cabin.

Thank you for your cooperation and assistance.

4 Depressurization

Ladies and gentlemen,

May I have your attention, please? Our plane is undergoing depressurization. Please keep calm and remain in your seat. You can find the oxygen mask that has dropped from the unit above your seat. Please reach up and pull the mask firmly toward your nose and mouth and slip the elastic band over your head, then the oxygen will automatically be supplied.

Thank you for your cooperation.

5 Bracing

Ladies and gentlemen,

For the sake of your safety, now we will explain three kinds of bracing positions against the impact of ditching.

First, keep the upper part of your body upright, grasp the arms of your seat with your hands firmly, and step on the floor with your feet firmly.

Second, cross your hands and place them behind your head, low your head as much as possible, step on the floor with your feet firmly.

Third, bend the upper part of your body forward as much as possible, separate your feet in a length as your shoulders, lower your head between your knees and clasp both ankles or brace both legs.

When instructed to brace for impact, please take this position so that the flight attendants can help you.

6 Words and phrases

instruct [ɪn'strʌkt] v. 教;命令;指导
waist [weɪst] n. 腰部;腰
illuminate [ɪ'lu:mɪneɪt] v. 照明
automatically [ˌɔ:tə'mætɪkli] adv. 自动地
flow B[fləʊ]/A[floʊ] n. 流动
elastic [ɪ'læstɪk] adj. 有弹性的
band [bænd] n. 带;箍
lead [li:d] v. 引导;带领
passenger safety card 乘客安全须知卡
advise [əd'vaɪz] v. 劝告;建议
minor ['maɪnə(r)] adj. 较小的;轻微的
undergo B[ˌʌndə'gəʊ]/A[ˌʌndər'goʊ] v. 经历;经受
depressurization B[di:ˌpreʃəraɪ'zeɪʃn]/A[di:ˌpreʃəraɪ'zeɪʃn] n. 降压;减压
oxygen B['ɒksɪdʒən]/A['ɑ:ksɪdʒən] n. 氧气;氧
unit ['ju:nɪt] n. 单元
ditching B['dɪtʃɪŋ]/A['dɪtʃɪŋ] n. 海上迫降

7 Notes to the announcements

(1) To put your vest on, simply slip it over your head, then fasten the buckles and pull the straps tightly around your waist.
将救生衣经头部穿好,并将带子由后向前在腰部扣好、系紧。

(2) Pull the mask firmly towards you to start the flow of oxygen.
用力向下拉面罩开始氧气供应。

(3) Place the mask over your nose and mouth and slip the elastic band over your head.

将面罩罩在口鼻处，把带子套在头上。

(4) Simply place the metal tip into the buckle and tighten the strap.

将金属片插入扣孔并拉紧安全带。

(5) In case of emergency, exit indications and track lighting will illuminate automatically leading you to the nearest exit.

在紧急情况下，客舱内所有的出口指示灯和通道指示灯会自动亮起，指引您从最近的出口撤离。

(6) First, keep the upper part of your body upright, grasp the arms of your seat with your hands firmly, and step on the floor with your feet firmly.

第一，上身挺直，双手用力抓住座椅扶手，双脚用力蹬地。

(7) Second, cross your hands and place them behind your head, low your head as much as possible, step on the floor with your feet firmly.

第二，两臂交叉置于头后，头尽量低下，双脚用力蹬地。

(8) Third, bend the upper part of your body forward as much as possible, separate your feet in a length as your shoulders, lower your head between your knees and clasp both ankles or brace both legs.

第三，身体尽量前倾，双脚分开，与肩同宽，头贴在双膝之间，双手抓紧脚踝或抱紧双腿。

Part Four Role Play

In small groups, make up a dialogue based on the following situations

(1) A passenger smokes in the lavatory and sets off the fire alarm. A cabin attendant is trying to deal with the problem.

(2) A passenger is afraid of emergency landing, and asks a cabin attendant for help.

(3) In an emergency landing, a passenger wants to inflate the life vest and put it on.

Part Five Exercises

1 Fill in the blanks in the following dialogues

Dialogue 1

CA: What can I do for you, madam?

PAX: ＿＿＿＿＿＿(1)＿＿＿＿＿＿(我能在哪里为我的孩子找到救生衣)?

CA: Please remain seated and keep your seat belt fastened. ＿＿＿＿＿＿(2)＿＿＿＿＿＿(我将从头顶行李架上为您取下救生衣).

PAX: Thank you.

CA：Just hold your baby and leave it to me. ＿＿＿＿＿＿＿＿（3）＿＿＿＿＿＿＿＿（一旦离开客舱,请拉下充气阀门）.

PAX：Can you tell me where I can find my life vest?

CA：Sure. ＿＿＿＿＿（4）＿＿＿＿＿（您的救生衣位于您的座椅下方）.

Dialogue 2

CA：Release your seat belts and get out now.

PAX1：Help, please. I can't release my seat belt!

CA：＿＿＿＿＿＿＿（5）＿＿＿＿＿＿＿（请向上扳起环扣,女士）.

PAX1：Thank you. I can release it now.

CA：You're welcome.

PAX2：Excuse me. ＿＿＿＿＿＿＿＿（6）＿＿＿＿＿＿＿＿（请帮我从头顶行李架里拿一下我的包,可以吗）?

CA：Leave your bags behind, go … go … go.

PAX2：I can't breathe, help me …

CA：Everyone kneels down on the floor and follows the emergency floor light. ＿＿＿＿＿＿＿＿（7）＿＿＿＿＿＿＿＿（它会引导你们去出口）!

PAX2：But I can't see anything.

CA：＿＿＿＿＿＿＿（8）＿＿＿＿＿＿＿（请抓紧您前方的那位旅客,女士,跟在他的身后前往出口处）. OK, jump … jump … go … go.

PAX2：My glasses … I need my glasses.

CA：＿＿＿＿＿＿＿（9）＿＿＿＿＿＿＿（请脱鞋,取下眼镜,女士）.

2 Translate the following phrases into English

(1) 防冲撞姿势　　　　　　　(2) 安全须知卡
(3) 紧急疏散　　　　　　　　(4) 紧急疏散软滑梯
(5) 尖锐物品　　　　　　　　(6) 客舱释压
(7) 紧急设备　　　　　　　　(8) 出口指示灯
(9) 机翼上方紧急出口　　　　(10) 紧急降落

3 Translate the following sentences into English

(1) 前舱厨房刚刚发生了一起小火灾。

(2) 机组人员会竭尽全力确保乘客的安全。

(3) 抓住前面座椅靠背,并将您的头放在双臂之间。

(4) 飞机着陆时,请保持"防冲撞姿势",直到飞机完全停稳。

(5) 我们的机长完全有信心安全着陆,机组所有人员都受过针对这种情形的良好的训练。

4 Translate the following sentences into Chinese

(1) Fasten your seatbelt immediately. The plane will make an emergency landing because of the sudden breakdown of an engine.

(2) Your life vest is located under your seat. It can only be used in case of a water landing.

(3) There are 8 emergency exits on this aircraft. Please locate the exit the nearest to you.

(4) Our aircraft is now experiencing strong turbulence, and it will last for some time. Please be seated and fasten your seat belt.

(5) On the command of "brace for impact", cross your hands and place them behind your head, then bend over, keep your head down, stay down.

5 Discussion

(1) What are the safety demonstration items in the cabin?

(2) Do you know how to explain the use of safety demonstration items to passengers?

Part Six Supplementary Reading

Text 1 Emergency Landing

An emergency landing is a prioritized landing made by an aircraft in response to an emergency which contains an imminent or on-going threat to the safety and operation of the aircraft or involves a sudden need for a passenger or crew on board to be on land such as a medical emergency.

Forced landing—the aircraft is forced to make a landing due to technical problems. Landing as soon as possible is a priority, no matter where, since a major system failure has occurred or is imminent. It is caused by the failure of or damage to vital systems such as engines, hydraulics, or landing gear, and so a landing must be attempted where a runway is needed but none is available.

The pilot is essentially trying to get the aircraft on the ground in a way which minimizes the possibility of injury or death to the people aboard. This means that the forced landing may even occur when the aircraft is still flyable, in order to prevent a crash or ditching situation.

Ditching is the same as a forced landing, only on water. After the disabled aircraft makes contact with the surface of the water, the aircraft will most likely sink if it is not designed to float, although it may float for hours, depending on damage.

Text 2 Cabin Fire

As for cabin fire, each airline has its own operation procedures and every flight attendant of every airlines has received strict training about how to deal with cabin fire. If a fire occurs on board, the cabin crew will try to put out the fire in the first place, and at the same time calm and take care of the passengers. If necessary, the cabin crew will evacuate passengers around the fire, but will avoid mass evacuation since the aircraft may be out of balance by mass evacuation. If the smoke is heavy, the cabin crew should inform passengers bending down and cover their noses and mouths using their sleeves. If conditions allow, give passengers bottles of water and inform them wetting any clothes or handkerchief and cover mouths with them.

When the fire has been put out, the cabin crew will decide whether to make an emergency landing or fly back according to the specific situations. The cabin crew will also arrange one flight attendant to monitor the fire spot, and arrange another flight attendant to calm passengers down. The cabin crew will do everything possible to ensure the safety of passengers until the plane makes a complete stop and all passengers have been evacuated safely.

Text 3 Turbulence

If you have been on a plane, the odds are that you've experienced some turbulence. Turbulence is that bumpy, choppy sensation you feel as the plane hits a rough air pocket. Turbulence can range from slight to severe bouncing, pitching and rolling. Even mild turbulence can shift objects in the overhead lockers and send drinks flying off tray tables. Severe turbulence can make walking difficult and send loose items flying about the cabin. You can be assured that the plane is built to withstand these conditions. However, severe turbulence can result in injuries.

Here are some strategies to protect passengers from the effects of turbulence:

Always wear your seat belt when seated;

Hold on the seat backs or overhead lockers when walking in the cabin;

Listen to all safety announcements carefully and follow cabin attendants' instructions;

Remain calm if turbulence occurs;

Be careful when opening the overhead lockers.

Decide whether the following statements are true (T) or false (F) according to the passage

(1) The plane will make an emergency landing because of the sudden breakdown of engine. (   )

(2) In the unlikely event of an aircraft having to emergency landing, you must adopt the brace position. (   )

(3) If there is a cabin fire, the cabin crew should evacuate passengers first, even mass evacuation. (   )

(4) Severe turbulence can make walking difficult and send loose items flying about the cabin. (   )

(5) Fasten the seat belt, hold on the seat backs and follow cabin attendants' safety instructions can protect passengers from turbulence. (   )

Module 5 Landing

Unit 15 Pre-arrival

Learning Objectives

1. Be familiar with various boarding dialogues and announcements.
2. Grasp relevant English expression.
3. Know how to make landing preparations.
4. Know the cabin attendants' responsibilities.

Part One Listening

1 Listen to the dialogue and choose the best answer to each question

(1) Does the passenger have to pay duty for the watches?
A. Yes, he does.
B. No, he doesn't.
C. Not mentioned in the dialogue.

(2) What will happen if the passenger doesn't list all taxable items?
A. He will pay heavy fines.
B. The Customs officials will let him pass.
C. He will have to pay duty for them.

(3) Where should the passenger go through the entry formalities?
A. On board
B. At the ticket counter
C. In the terminal building

听力音频

2 Listen to the following dictation and fill in the blanks with exact words or phrases

Filling Form before Landing

Ladies and gentlemen,

We will be landing at Frankfurt airport shortly. Before you _____(1)_____ Customs and Immigration, it is _____(2)_____ for you to _____(3)_____ the forms required by the French Government. In order to _____(4)_____ your passage through Customs and Immigration, we will be _____(5)_____ the forms to you, and you can _____(6)_____ them before we land. If you have any questions about completing the forms, please ask a cabin attendant for help. They will be very happy to _____(7)_____ you. Thank you.

Part Two　Dialogues

CA: cabin attendant　PAX: passenger

1 Dialogue 1

CA: Excuse me. Would you please switch your laptop computer off? We will be landing in a few minutes.
PAX: I'm dealing with an urgent assignment. I promise I'll switch it off in five minutes.
CA: I can understand that, madam. But when the plane is going to land, all the electric devices should be switched off to comply with the regulations.
PAX: All right, Miss. I'll switch it off right away.

2 Dialogue 2

CA: Excuse me, sir. Would you please fill out these forms before we get to Bangkok?
PAX: Why do we have to fill out the forms on board?
CA: You'd better do so if you want to shorten the time going through Customs, Immigration and Quarantine.
PAX: All right. When do I have to return them to you?
CA: Just place them inside your passport. Then hand them in to the Customs officials.
PAX: I see. Oh, I can't find my entry card.
CA: You mean you lost it? No worries. I'll bring you another one.
PAX: Thank you.

3 Dialogue 3

CA: Excuse me, Miss. Would you please fill out this Customs form for the declaration of your luggage?
PAX: Should I list all taxable items, including my personal effects?
CA: I'm afraid so. All dutiable items which are not found on the declaration form may subject the owner to heavy fines.
PAX: Well, I've got some cosmetics with me. They are gifts for my friends. Do I have to declare it?
CA: How many do you have?

PAX: 4 lipsticks and 3 bottles of nourishing cream, and I've got 2 bottles of perfume.
CA: I guess the Customs officials will let them pass.
PAX: Thank you very much for your information.
CA: If you have any difficulties in filling in the form, please let me know.
PAX: Sure.

4 Dialogue 4

PAX: Excuse me, can I ask you something if you are available right now?
CA: Sure, go ahead.
PAX: You see, this is my first international flight ever. I heard that the airport procedures are quite complicated after we arrive. Can you tell me what to do after we land?
CA: Oh, yeah. Are you travelling as a tourist?
PAX: Yes.
CA: The first thing is to go through Immigration. Follow the crowds to the Immigration windows after we land. There you'll be asked questions as why you come to the US and how long and where you are going to stay. So get the information ready now. At San Francisco Airport, tourist visas are accepted at the windows on the right and citizens and green card holders on the left. So queue at right lines.
PAX: OK.
CA: Then you collect your luggage at the carousel. Let me see which number that would be ... Ah, it's number 26.
PAX: Is it easy to find?
CA: I think so. Go downstairs after you go through the Immigration. There are a few giant carousels with numbers on top. You won't miss it.
PAX: Great! Is there a taxi service outside of the terminal?
CA: I'm afraid you'll have to book it in advance.
PAX: Oh, I didn't know ... Maybe there are shuttle buses?
CA: That, too. But you still need reservations. Maybe you can try some public transportation. There are light rails connecting the airport with nearby cities.
PAX: Sounds good to me!

5 Dialogue 5

(A passenger sees the aileron bending down before the aircraft descends. She shouts to one of the CAs.)
PAX: Oh, my God! We are going to crash! Stewardess! Stewardess!
CA: Yes, here I am, madam. What's the matter?
PAX: The wing is broken. We gonna crash! I saw it!
CA: I don't see what you mean, madam. Would you please show me the broken part?
PAX: OK. It's there on the left wing. The rear part bent and I heard the noise. I think

it is going to drop down!

CA: I don't think so, madam. It's the aileron. You know, when the airplane is descending it will drop down. This is aerodynamics. There's nothing to worry about. Believe me.

PAX: Are you sure? If that's the case, then I'm sorry for the fuss.

CA: I'm sure, madam. I hope you are all right now.

PAX: Can you bring me a cup of coffee, please? I need coffee to calm myself down.

CA: I'm sorry, madam. We are landing now. Nothing is served at this time, I'm afraid.

6 Words and expressions

assignment [ə'saɪnmənt] *n.* 分配；任务；作业；功课

quarantine B['kwɒrəntiːn]/A['kwɔːrəntiːn] *n.* 检疫隔离期；隔离；检疫；检疫区，隔离区 *v.* 对（动物或人）进行隔离检疫

official [ə'fɪʃl] *adj.* 官方的；正式的；公务的 *n.* 官员；公务员；高级职员

entry card 入境卡，登记卡

declaration [ˌdekləˈreɪʃn] *n.* （纳税品等的）申报；宣布；公告；申诉书

taxable ['tæksəbl] *adj.* 应纳税的；可征税的

personal effects 个人财产；所有物，私物

dutiable B['djuːtɪəbl]/A['djuːtɪəbl] *adj.* 应纳税的；应征税的；（输入品）应课关税的

nourishing B['nʌrɪʃɪŋ]/A['nɜːrɪʃɪŋ] *adj.* 有营养的；滋养多的 *v.* 滋养；养育

queue [kjuː] *n.* 队列；长队；辫子 *v.* 排队；排队等候

carousel [ˌkærəˈsel] *n.* 旋转木马；行李传送带；轮播

terminal B['tɜːmɪnl]/A['tɜːrmɪnl] *n.* 航空站；终点站；终端机 *adj.* 晚期的；无可挽回的；末端的；终点的；期末的

rear B[rɪə(r)]/A[rɪr] *n.* 后面；后部；屁股 *adj.* 后方的，后面的；后部的 *v.* 抚养；培养；喂养，饲养；栽种，培植；（马等动物）用后腿直立；竖起

aileron B['eɪlərɒn]/A['eɪləraːn] *n.* 副翼

aerodynamics B[ˌeərəʊdaɪˈnæmɪks]/A[ˌeroʊdaɪˈnæmɪks] *n.* 空气动力（特性）；空气动力

7 Notes to the dialogues

(1) But when the plane is going to land, all the electric devices should be switched off to comply with the regulations.

但当飞机准备下降时，根据规定，所有电子设备都必须关闭。

(2) You'd better do so if you want to shorten the time going through Customs, Immigration and Quarantine.

如果您想要缩短通关、入境和检疫的时间，最好这么做。

(3) All dutiable items which are not found on the declaration form may subject the owner to heavy fines.

所有未在申报表格上发现的应课税物品，都可令物主被处以重罚。

(4) It's the aileron. You know, when the airplane is descending it will drop down.

This is aerodynamics. There's nothing to worry about. Believe me.

那是副翼。当飞机下降时,它也会下降。这符合空气动力学,没什么好担心的。请相信我。

Part Three Announcements

1 30 minutes before landing

Ladies and gentlemen,

We will be arriving at Beijing International airport in 30 minutes. As we are landing shortly, please put your seat back upright, secure your tray-table (footrest) and put your armrest down. Please make sure that your seat belt is securely fastened, and your window shades are drawn up. In order not to interfere with our flight systems, all electronic devices including your laptops must be switched off now. You are also reminded that all mobile phones must remain switched off until doors are open. We will be turning off in-flight entertainment systems shortly. The lavatories will be closed in a short while.

广播音频

2 Quarantine and customs

Ladies and gentlemen,

According to the Quarantine regulations of America, passengers may not bring in fresh fruits, cut flowers, meat, dairy products or other animal/ plant products. Passengers who are in possession of such items are kindly requested to dispose of them or present them to your flight attendants prior to landing. The Customs of America requires that passengers carrying articles and currencies exceeding the Customs allowance must declare with the Customs officials. Please complete the Customs Declaration Form and hand it in to the Customs officials.

Thank you.

3 Filling out the entry forms

Ladies and gentlemen,

Your attention, please. We're soon landing at Beijing Capital International Airport. Since Beijing is an entry port of China, all the passengers on board, including kids, should fill in an arrival card and a Customs Declaration Form. And you should complete the forms before landing. The forms will be distributed soon. We'll help you if you have any difficulty.

4 Words and expressions

secure B[sɪˈkjʊə(r)]/A[səˈkjʊr] *adj.* 安全的;无虑的;有把握的;稳固的 *v.* 保护;获得;拴牢

interfere B[ˌɪntəˈfɪə(r)]/A[ˌɪntərˈfɪr] *v.* 干涉;妨碍;干预;冲突;介入

exceeding [ɪkˈsiːdɪŋ] v. 超过（某数量）；超越，越出（限制）（exceed 的现在分词）

distributed B[dɪsˈtrɪbjuːtɪd]/A[dɪˈstrɪbjuːtɪd] v. 分配；分发（distribute 的过去分词）

5 Notes to the announcements

（1）As we are landing shortly, please put your seat back upright, secure your tray-table (footrest) and put your armrest down. Please make sure that your seat belt is securely fastened, and your window shades are drawn up.

由于我们马上就要着陆了，请您收起您的座椅靠背，固定好您的小桌板（脚踏），放下您的扶手。请确认您的安全带已系紧，遮光板已拉上。

（2）According to the Quarantine regulations of America, passengers may not bring in fresh fruits, cut flowers, meat, dairy products or other animal/ plant products.

根据美国检疫规定，入境旅客不得携带新鲜水果、鲜切花、肉类、奶制品及动植物产品。

（3）The Customs of America requires that passengers carrying articles and currencies exceeding the Customs allowance must declare with the Customs officials.

美国海关要求旅客在携带超过海关限额的物品或现金时，必须向海关职员申报。

Part Four　Role Play

In small groups, make up a dialogue based on the following situations

（1）A passenger asks whether it is necessary to fill in CIQ forms on board. And he asks for entry cards in Spanish. Help him complete those forms and cards.

（2）A passenger who is travelling from Shanghai to Chicago takes some meat product for his son. Explain to him that they are not allowed to enter America and help him to dispose of them.

Part Five　Exercise

1 Spell the words with the help of their definitions and first letters

（1）d_____ to make due statement of goods for duty

（2）d_____ to put in a particular or suitable place

（3）l_____ a distilled or spirituous beverage, as brandy or whisky

（4）s_____ affected greatly or easily by sth

（5）d_____ to pass out or deliver (forms, mail, newspapers, etc.) to passengers

（6）d_____ a specific tax imposed by law on the import or export of goods

（7）c_____ a powder, lotion, lipstick, rouge, or other preparation for beautifying the face, skin, hair, nails, etc.

（8）f_____ compliance with formal rules

（9）a_____ a thing

(10) o_____ person who holds a public officer

2 Translate the following phrases into English

(1) 个人物品　　　　　　　(2) 入境旅客
(3) 现金　　　　　　　　　(4) 新鲜水果
(5) 海关职员　　　　　　　(6) 应纳税商品
(7) 海关申报单　　　　　　(8) 虫害
(9) 重罚　　　　　　　　　(10) 垃圾桶

3 Translate the following sentences into English

(1) 您可以在我们到达北京之前填写这些表格吗？
(2) 您需按要求在降落前填写通关、入境和检疫表格。
(3) 应纳税的商品如果没有列在申报单上，会被处以很重的罚金。
(4) 每位乘客允许免税携带200支香烟或50支雪茄或250克烟丝。
(5) 根据美国检疫要求，入境旅客不得携带新鲜水果。

4 Translate the following sentences into Chinese

(1) Passengers who are in possession of such items are kindly requested to dispose of them or present them to your flight attendants prior to landing.

(2) In order to speed up the arrival formalities in the airport, you're requested to fill in the forms for Customs, Immigration and Quarantine before landing.

(3) Since Beijing is an entry port of China, all the passengers on board, including kids, should fill in an arrival card and a Customs Declaration Form.

(4) If you are unsure about anything else, please read carefully the list of articles that need to be declared on the back of the form.

(5) All my family members are on board. Can we fill in one Customs Declaration Form?

Part Six　Supplementary Reading

ICQ

Immigration

The first stop after deboarding the aircraft in another country is immigration. Everyone is required by law to pass through Immigration and Customs. Holders of the country's passports and permanent residences are directed to one particular area, whilst international visitors are directed to another.

Customs

Passengers must have their passports and other travel documents ready to go through the Customs.

In the majority of airports all over the world, there are normally two exits through the Customs.

A green channel if passengers have nothing to declare.

A red channel if passengers have goods to declare.

A blue channel existing in European countries is for passengers who are travelling from an airport within the European Union, where luggage has already been cleared through Customs control.

The passengers must declare all food, plant material or animal products within their possession. If the passengers are not sure about their declaration, they may ask a Customs officer for advice. It is in the passengers, own interest to be completely honest with Customs officials at all times as false or misleading information (e. g. false receipts) will lead to severe penalties, which may result in goods being taken, heavy fines imposed and in the worst case, imprisonment.

Even when a passenger passes through the green channel, the Customs officer has the authority to ask him or her to open his or her luggage for checking. At some airports, bags going through this channel are x-rayed to ensure that Quarantine and Customs are being enforced.

When passengers proceed through the red channel, they will be asked to declare certain items, for example, items of value, food, alcohol and cigarettes. If the passengers are found to be carrying more than the allowance, they will be required to pay duty or tax on those items.

The following are typical examples of Customs Duty-free Allowance in the majority of airports all over the world.

Duty-free Allowance for UK from outside Europe

- 200 cigarettes;
- 2 liters of still table wine;
- 1 liter of spirits or strong liqueurs over 22% volume; or 2 liters of fortified wine, sparkling wine or other liqueurs.
- 60 cc/mL of perfume;
- 250 cc/mL of toilet water;

Duty-free Allowance for China

- 400 cigarettes if staying under 6 months;
- 600 cigarettes if staying over 6 months;
- 2 bottles each not exceeding 0.75 liter for stay less than 6 months;
- 4 bottles each not exceeding 0.75 liter for stay more than 6 months;
- Reasonable quantity of perfume for personal use.

Duty-free Allowance for USA

- 200 cigarettes;
- 1 liter of alcoholic beverage.

Quarantine

Almost all airports of the world have quarantine areas and entry regulations upon arrival into the country. The following procedure is in place for passengers who fly into some airports.

Upon arrival, one of the first checks a passenger has to pass is the Quarantine check. At the checkpoint, he or she will be required to show his or her passport and visa and fill in a health declaration form. Anyone with the listed diseases such as yellow fever, cholera, VD, leprosy, infectious pulmonary tuberculosis, AIDS or symptoms of SARS will be prohibited. Those coming from the areas with epidemic yellow fever must show their valid certificates of inoculation against this disease. Those with symptoms of fever, diarrhea, vomiting or rashes must declare this information accurately.

If a passenger is showing any of the above symptoms upon arrival at an airport, they are liable to be quarantined for an unspecific period of time or until their condition improves significantly enough for them to carry on with their journey.

Choose the correct answer to the following questions

(1) What is the first stop for passengers who get off the aircraft in another country?
A. Immigration   B. Immigration and Customs
C. Customs   D. Quarantine

(2) Which of the following is NOT true about the Customs channels?
A. A green channel is for passengers who have nothing to declare.
B. A red channel is for passengers who have duty-free goods to declare.
C. A blue channel exists in European countries.
D. A blue channel is for passengers who are travelling from an airport within the European Union.

(3) Which of the following is true about the Customs declaration?
A. Passengers don't have to declare animal products within their possession.
B. Passengers who pass through the green channel don't have to open their luggage for checking.
C. Passengers who go through the red channel should declare food, alcohol and cigarettes.
D. If the passenger is carrying more than the allowance, they will have a tax exemption.

(4) If passengers have _____ , they will be prohibited to go into the country.
A. yellow fever, cholera
B. VD, leprosy
C. infectious pulmonary tuberculosis, SARS
D. all the above

Unit 16 Landing and Farewell

Learning Objectives

1. Be familiar with various landing dialogues and announcements.
2. Grasp relevant English expressions.
3. Know how to do the farewell.
4. Know the cabin attendants' responsibilities.

Part One Listening

1 Listen to the dialogue and choose the best answer to each question

(1) What's the time now?

A. 6:10 p.m.

B. 6:30 p.m.

C. 6:45 p.m.

(2) How can the passenger find the Baggage Claim Area?

A. The flight attendant will help her to the place.

B. The ground staff will take her there.

C. The signs at the arrival hall will lead her there.

(3) What does the passenger think of the service during the flight?

A. She is very satisfied with the service.

B. She thinks it is unpleasant to be served at this flight.

C. She makes no comments on the service.

2 Listen to the following dialogue and fill in the blanks

CA: cabin attendant   PAX: passenger

PAX: Miss, when are we going to arrive in Beijing?

CA: We'll arrive there in 20 minutes. The arrival time is ____(1)____ a.m.

PAX: I've lost ____(2)____ completely. I wonder how I adjust my watch to Beijing time.

CA: It's 8 o'clock in the morning now. New York is ____(3)____ hours ahead of Beijing but one day behind.

PAX: What's the weather like there?

CA: According to the ____(4)____, it's sunny and the ____(5)____ is 32 degrees Centigrade.

PAX: Terrific.

CA: I hope you'll have a nice stay in Beijing.

Part Two   Dialogues

CA: cabin attendant   PAX: passenger

1 Dialogue 1

(A cabin attendant is helping a senior passenger to disembark.)

CA: Excuse me, sir. Would you please let this old granny go first?

PAX1: Sure. Please!

CA: Thank you, sir. It's so kind of you to make way for this senior passenger.

PAX1: Not at all.

CA: (To the old lady.) Madam, please watch your step. It's raining and very slippery outside.

PAX2: Thanks. You are so thoughtful.

CA: See you, madam. I hope you will have a good time here!

PAX2: I will. Thank you.

2 Dialogue 2

PAX1: Hello, Miss.

CA: (To a disabled passenger.) Yes, what can I do for you?

PAX1: I need some assistance to get off the plane. Can you help me?

CA: Of course, but would you please wait a minute? I'll get somebody to help you. Oh, sir. Have you got a wheelchair booked for getting off?

PAX1: I do indeed.

CA: Great. Well, just hold on and I'll be back as soon as possible.

PAX1: No problem.

CA: Here's your wheelchair, sir. Have a nice day!

PAX1: Many thanks.

CA: (To an elderly passenger.) Would you like me to help you there, madam?

PAX2: Yes, please. I can't unfasten this belt. I'm so sorry about this.

CA: Let me have a look. There you go, madam. Here let me give you a hand getting up.

PAX2: Thank you, dear.

CA: Have you got any hand baggage with you?

PAX2: Yes, it's just over there.

CA: Let me get it for you.

对话音频

PAX2: Thank you. Oh, my legs are feeling awfully tired.

CA: Do you have a wheelchair booked for getting off?

PAX2: No, I don't.

CA: Just take a seat there for a moment and I'll try to organize one for you.

PAX2: Thank you, dear.

CA: You're welcome.

3 Dialogue 3

PAX: Excuse me.

CA: Yes? May I help you?

PAX: My ears feel funny. I can't hear properly.

CA: Please calm down. It's because of the change in air pressure. You may feel better if you try chewing gums or swallowing.

PAX: Really? Let me try. But it seems doesn't work. My ears still hurt so much.

CA: Don't worry. Let's try another way. Make a deep breath. Hold your nose and blow like this. How do you feel now?

PAX: Oh, I feel much better now. Thank you.

CA: Now you can be easy to stay in your seat. We're landing.

PAX: Thanks for your help.

CA: Anytime.

4 Dialogue 4

PAX: Miss, is the plane going to arrive in Beijing on schedule?

CA: Yes, I think so.

PAX: What's the weather like there?

CA: According to the weather report, it's raining there.

PAX: How annoying! Is it raining hard?

CA: Well, no. There's only a light rain on and off.

PAX: Is is going to be all right for landing?

CA: Yes, of course. The visibility is not so poor. Please don't worry.

PAX: Thank you for telling me all these.

CA: Thank you for flying with us and hope to see you again.

5 Dialogue 5

CA: Madam, our plane will be landing at Guangzhou Baiyun Airport very soon.

PAX: Thank you for everything you've done for me during the flight. It's been a comfortable flight.

CA: I'm glad you've enjoyed the flight. We do hope you will enjoy your stay in China.

PAX: Definitely. I'll try to get myself adapted to the life in China.

CA: Are you sure nothing is left behind?

PAX: Yes, I have everything with me.

CA: We look forward to serving you again in the future.

PAX: It certainly will. This is a present for you.

CA: That's very kind of you. I accept your kindness, but please forgive me for not taking your gift. I was only doing my job.

PAX: Your service was splendid! I will choose your airlines for my next trip.

CA: I'm glad to hear that. Goodbye and good luck!

PAX: Goodbye!

6 Words and expressions

senior ['siːniə(r)] adj. 高级水平的；(父子同名时，加在父亲的名字前)老；大；级别(或地位)高的 n. 上司；较年长者；毕业班学生

slippery ['slɪpəri] adj. 滑的；油滑的；滑得站不稳的

disabled [dɪs'eɪbld] adj. 残疾的；有缺陷的；(设施等)为残疾人设计的 v. 使失去能力(disable 的过去式和过去分词)

wheelchair B['wiːltʃeə(r)]/A['wiːltʃer] n. 轮椅

indeed [ɪn'diːd] adv. 的确；真正地；(强调肯定的答复等)

properly B['prɒpəli]/A['prɑːpərli] adv. 适当地；正确地；恰当地

pressure ['preʃə(r)] n. 压力 v. 迫使

chewing ['tʃuːɪŋ] v. 咀嚼；嚼碎；(因紧张等)不停地啃(chew 的现在分词) n. 嚼

swallowing B[s'wɒləʊɪŋ]/A[s'wɑːloʊɪŋ] v. 吞下；咽下(swallow 的现在分词)

annoying [ə'nɔɪɪŋ] adj. 讨厌的；恼人的

visibility [ˌvɪzə'bɪləti] n. 能见度；可见性；能见距离；明显性

definitely ['defɪnətli] adv. 清楚地；当然；明确地；肯定地

adapted [ə'dæptɪd] adj. 适合……的 v. 使适应；改编

splendid ['splendɪd] adj. 壮丽的；雄伟的；极佳的；非常好的

7 Notes to the dialogues

(1) Please watch your step.

请注意脚下。

(2) Here let me give you a hand getting up.

我给你搭把手帮你起身。

(3) My ears feel funny.

我的耳朵难受。

(4) I can't hear properly.

我完全听不见。

(5) There's only a light rain on and off.

只有小雨，时下时停。

(6) I accept your kindness, but please forgive me for not taking your gift.

我接受您的好意，但请原谅我不能接受您的礼物。

Part Three Announcements

1 Landing with possible transfer

Ladies and gentlemen,

We have landed at Chongqing Jiangbei Airport. The local time is 1:00 p.m. The ground temperature is 24 degrees Centigrade or 75 degrees Fahrenheit.

Please remain in your seat until the "Fasten Seat Belt" sign is turned off. Be careful when opening the overhead locker.

If you have an onward flight, you should go to the transit desk in the airport.

Thank you.

2 Landing

Ladies and gentlemen,

Welcome to Guangzhou. According to the latest weather report, the outside temperature is 20 degrees Centigrade, or 68 degrees Fahrenheit.

Our plane is still taxiing. For your safety, please stay in your seat for the time being. When the aircraft stops completely and the "Fasten Seat Belt" Sign is turned off, please detach the seat belt and take all your carry-on items and passport to complete the entry formalities in the terminal. Please be careful when retrieving items from the overhead compartment. Your checked baggage may be claimed at the baggage claim area at the arrival terminal.

3 Landing formalities

Ladies and gentlemen,

Welcome to Wuhan. Please take your passport and all your personal belongings when disembarking and complete the entry and quarantine formalities at the terminal. Your checked baggage may be claimed at No. 6 Baggage Claim. If you have any items to declare, please proceed to the Declaration Counter of the Customs.

If you have a domestic connecting flight, according to the Regulations of the Customs of the People's Republic of China, you need to claim your checked baggage and proceed through the Customs for the clearance of both your carry-on baggage and checked baggage. Then please go through the interline baggage procedures at the domestic transfer counter.

If you have an international connecting flight, please proceed to the international transit counter for further information or transit services.

See you next time and have a nice day!

Thank you!

4 Words and expressions

Centigrade ['sentɪgreɪd] *adj.* 摄氏温度的；百分度的

transit desk 中转站；中转台

detach [dɪ'tætʃ] *v.* 分离；派遣；使脱离

retrieving [rɪ'triːvɪŋ] *v.* 取回；索回；检索数据；挽回；找回（retrieve 的现在分词）

baggage claim area 行李认领处；取行李处；行李认领区

domestic [də'mestɪk] *adj.* 国内的；家庭的；驯养的 *n.* 佣人

5 Notes to the announcements

(1) Our plane is still taxiing.

我们的飞机正在跑道上滑行。

(2) When the aircraft stops completely and the "Fasten Seat Belt" Sign is turned off, please detach the seat belt and take all your carry-on items and passport to complete the entry formalities in the terminal.

当飞机完全停稳、安全带指示灯熄灭时，请解开安全带，整理好手提物品和护照，前往航站楼办理入境手续。

(3) If you have a domestic connecting flight, according to the Regulations of the Customs of the People's Republic of China, you need to claim your checked baggage and proceed through the Customs for the clearance of both your carry-on baggage and checked baggage.

如果你要搭乘国内中转航班，根据中国海关规定，你需要领取托运行李，然后在海关对托运和手提行李办理清关手续。

Part Four Role Play

In small groups, make up a dialogue based on the following situations

(1) The plane will be landing at the destination airport in about 40 minutes. Tell the passengers to prepare for landing. The weather is sunny, so you are going to arrive on schedule. However, you have to wait for the air bridge to put in position.

(2) A passenger is in a hurry to deplane to catch his connecting flight. Try to comfort him and tell him the relevant rules before the plane comes to a complete stop.

Part Five Exercises

1 Spell the words with the help of their definitions and first letters

(1) v_____ the distance one can see as determined by light and weather conditions

(2) s_____ of or for older or more experienced people

(3) a＿＿＿＿ to adjust oneself to different conditions, environment, etc

(4) d＿＿＿＿ (of a person) having a physical or mental condition that limits their movements, senses, or activities

(5) r＿＿＿＿ get sth back

(6) o＿＿＿＿ take responsibility for providing or arranging

(7) d＿＿＿＿ to unfasten and separate

(8) w＿＿＿＿ a chair fitted with wheels for use as a means of transport by a person who is unable to walk as a result of illness, injury, or disability

(9) f＿＿＿＿ say or feel that one is no longer angry about

(10) d＿＿＿＿ of or relating to one's own or a particular country

2 Translate the following phrases into English

(1) 廊桥
(2) 转机柜台
(3) 行李提取
(4) 失去时间感
(5) 客舱服务
(6) 到达大厅
(7) 能见度
(8) 天气预报
(9) 随身携带的物品
(10) 联运行李；转机行李

3 Translate the following sentences into English

(1) 你有没有预订下飞机用的轮椅？
(2) 你确定没有东西落下吗？
(3) 您可以试着嚼口香糖或者吞咽，感觉会好一些。
(4) 能见度不差。
(5) 我们期待未来再次为您服务。

4 Translate the following sentences into Chinese

(1) Be careful when opening the overhead locker.

(2) Your checked baggage may be claimed at the baggage claim area at the arrival terminal.

(3) If you have an international connecting flight, please proceed to the international transit counter for further information or transit services.

(4) Please take your passport and all your personal belongings when disembarking and complete the entry and quarantine formalities at the terminal.

(5) Please disembark from the front entry door and go over the air bridge.

Part Six Supplementary Reading

Landing and Jet Lag Disorder

If a passenger is arriving, he or she needs to have his or her passport and Incoming Passenger Card ready for clearance. His or her documents will be returned to him or her after processing. The passenger may then collect his or her luggage from the luggage hall and proceed to the baggage examination area.

Passengers are asked to remain seated until the plane taxis up to the jet way and stops. They will get out of their seats once the plane stops and they will get their carry-on baggage. The doors to the plane will not open until the jet way is ready to connect to the plane's fuselage. This will take a few minutes and at the same time, passengers have filled the aisles and wait impatiently until the First Class passengers and those needing assistance leave the plane first. As the passengers leave the plane, the flight attendants station themselves at the door to assist any passengers needing help. They smile and say "Thank you" or they will merely smile and say "Bye".

But another problem also confuses on some international passengers after a long-haul travel, as the airplanes can reach your destination in a comparable short time, they may have trouble with a jet leg disorder.

Jet lag, also called jet lag disorder, is a temporary sleep problem that can affect anyone who quickly travels across multiple time zones.

Your body has its own internal clock, or circadian rhythms, that signals your body when to stay awake and when to sleep. Jet lag occurs because your body's clock is still synced to your original time zone, instead of to the time zone where you've travelled. The more time zones crossed, the more likely you are to experience the jet lag.

Jet lag can cause daytime fatigue, an unwell feeling, difficulty staying alert and gastrointestinal problems. Jet lag is temporary, but it can significantly reduce your vacation or business travel comfort. Fortunately, there are steps you can take to help prevent or minimize the jet lag.

Symptoms of jet lag can vary. You may experience only one symptom or you may have many. Jet lag symptoms may include:

Disturbed sleep—such as insomnia, early waking or excessive sleepiness;

Daytime fatigue;

Have Difficulty in concentrating or functioning at your usual level;

Stomach problems, constipation or diarrhea;

A general feeling of not being well;

Mood changes;

Symptoms worse the farther you travel.

Jet lag symptoms usually occur within a day or two of travel if you've travelled across at least two time zones. Symptoms are likely to be worse or last longer the more time zones that you've crossed, especially if you travel in an easterly direction. It usually takes about a day to recover for each time zone crossed.

When to see a doctor

Jet lag is temporary. But if you're a frequent traveler and continually struggle with the jet lag, you may benefit from seeing a sleep specialist.

Decide whether the following statements are true (T) or false (F) according to the passage

(1) After arrival, the passenger may collect his luggage at the baggage claim area. (   )

(2) The cabin doors will open when the air bridge is connected to the plane. (   )

(3) Jet lag is an eternal sleep problem that affects passenger who travels across time zones. (   )

(4) Jet lag can cause daytime tiredness, a sick feeling and upset in stomach. (   )

(5) Passengers should go to see the doctor if their mood change. (   )

附录 A　世界各国主要航空公司代码

世界主要航空公司及二字代码

航空公司名称	两字代码	航空公司名称	两字代码
中国国际航空公司	CA	中国南方航空公司	CZ
中国东方航空公司	MU	厦门航空公司	MF
四川航空公司	3U	山东航空公司	SC
深圳航空公司	ZH	鹰联航空公司	EU
海南航空公司	HU	大新华航空公司	CN
上海航空公司	FM	华夏航空公司	G5
首都航空公司	JD	天津航空公司	GS
首都航空公司	8L	春秋航空公司	9C
长荣航空公司	BR	河南航空公司	VD
中华航空公司	CI	吉祥航空公司	HO
中国联合航空公司	KN	香港航空公司	HX
全日空航空公司	NH	港龙航空公司	KA
日本航空公司	JL	国泰航空公司	CX
日本跨洋航空公司	NU	澳门航空公司	NX
日本亚洲航空公司	EG	美国西北航空公司	NW
大韩航空公司	KE	美国联合航空公司	UA
韩亚航空公司	OZ	美国航空公司	AA
朝鲜民航公司	JS	联邦快递公司	FX
巴西航空公司	RG	美国大陆航空公司	CO
曼谷航空公司	PG	英国中部航空公司	BD
泰国航空公司	TG	英国航空公司	BA
印度尼西亚鹰航空公司	GA	德国汉莎航空公司	LH
瑞士航空公司	SR	法国航空公司	AF
卡塔尔航空公司	QR	意大利航空公司	AZ
希腊奥林匹克航空公司	OA	加拿大航空公司	AC
新加坡航空公司	SQ	新西兰航空公司	NZ
阿联酋航空公司	EK	澳洲航空公司	AO
乌兹别克斯坦航空公司	HY	南非航空公司	SA

续表

世界主要航空公司及二字代码			
蒙古航空公司	OM	科威特航空公司	KU
印度航空公司	IC	荷兰皇家航空公司	KL
西班牙航空公司	IB	马耳他航空公司	KM
葡萄牙航空公司	NI	肯尼亚航空公司	KQ
卢森堡航空公司	LG	芬兰航空公司	AY
捷克斯洛伐克航空公司	OK	哈萨克斯坦航空公司	K4
俄罗斯航空公司	SU	北欧航空公司	SK
奥地利航空公司	OS	以色列航空公司	LY

附录 B　世界主要城市及三字代码

Codes of Cities

世界主要城市及三字代码

城市英文名称	城市三字代码	城市中文名称	所属国家
ALBURY	ABX	阿尔伯里	澳大利亚
AUCKLAND	AKL	奥克兰	新西兰
AMSTERDAM	AMS	阿姆斯特丹	荷兰
ANK ARA	ANK	安哥拉	土耳其
STOCKHOLM	ARN	斯德哥尔摩	瑞典
ATLANTA	ATL	亚特兰大	美国
ATHENS	ATH	雅典	希腊
ABU DHABI	AUH	阿布扎比	阿联酋
BERLIN	BER	柏林	德国
BANGOR	BGR	邦哥尔	美国
BEIJING	BJS	北京	中国
BANGKOK	BKK	曼谷	泰国
BRISBANE	BNE	布里斯班	澳大利亚
BOMBAY	BOM	孟买	印度
BUENOS AIRES	BUE	布宜诺斯艾利斯	阿根廷
COLUMBIA	CAE	哥伦比亚	美国
CAIRO	CAI	开罗	埃及
GUANGZHOU	CAN	广州	中国
CHIANG RAI	CEI	清莱	泰国
ZHENGZHOU	CGO	郑州	中国
ROME	CHII	芝加哥	美国
ROME	CIA	罗马	意大利
CHEJU	CJU	济州	韩国
COPENHAGEN	CPH	哥本哈根	丹麦
CAPE TOWN	CPT	开普敦	南非
CHENGDU	CTU	成都	中国
WASHINGTON	DCA	华盛顿	美国

续表

世界主要城市及三字代码			
DENVER	DEN	丹佛	美国
DALIAN	DLC	大连	中国
DUSSELDORF	DUS	杜塞尔多夫	德国
DUBAI	DXB	迪拜	阿联酋
DETROIT	DTT	底特律	美国
ANKARA	ESB	安卡拉	土耳其
FRANKFURT	FRA	法兰克福	德国
FUKUOK A	FUK	福冈	日本
GENEVA	GVA	日内瓦	瑞士
HANOI	HAN	河内	越南
HEL SINKI	HEL	赫尔辛基	芬兰
HANGZHOU	HGH	杭州	中国
HIROSHIMA	HIJ	广岛	日本
HONG KONG	HKG	香港	中国
PHUKET	HKT	普吉岛	泰国
JAK ARTA	JKT	雅加达	印尼
HARBIN	HRB	哈尔滨	中国
HAVRE	HVR	哈佛	美国
KIEV	IEV	基辅	乌克兰
JOHANNESBURG	JNB	约翰内斯堡	南非
KILIMANJARO	JRO	乞力马扎罗	坦桑尼亚
KAOHSIUNG	KHH	高雄	中国
KUNMING	KMG	昆明	中国
KUALA LUMPUR	KUL	吉隆坡	马来西亚
KAZAN	KZN	喀山	俄罗斯
LOS ANGELES	LAX	洛杉矶	美国
LONDON	LON	伦敦	英国
ST PETERSBURG	LED	圣彼得堡	俄罗斯
LIMA	LIM	利马	秘鲁
LUXEMBOURG	LUX	卢森堡	卢森堡
MADRID	MAD	马德里	西班牙
MILAN	MIL	米兰	意大利
MIAMI	MIA	迈阿密	美国
MOSCOW	MOW	莫斯科	俄罗斯

续表

世界主要城市及三字代码			
MAURITIUS	MRU	毛里求斯	毛里求斯
MARSEILE	MRS	马赛	法国
NANCHONG	NAO	南昌	中国
NAIROBI	NBO	内罗毕	肯尼亚
NANJING	NKG	南京	中国
NEW YORK	NYC	纽约	美国
ORLANDO	ORL	奥兰多	美国
OSAKA	OSA	大阪	日本
PARIS	PAR	巴黎	法国
PERTH	PER	珀斯	澳大利亚
PHNOM	PNH	金边	柬埔寨
RIO DE JANEIRO	RIO	里约热内卢	巴西
ROME	ROM	罗马	意大利
SAO PAULO	SAO	圣保罗	巴西
SANTIAGO	SCL	圣地亚哥	智利
SEATTLE	SEA	西雅图	美国
SEOUL	SEL	釜山	韩国
SAN FRANCISCO	SFO	旧金山	美国
HO CHI MINH CITY	SGN	胡志明市	越南
SHANGHAI	SHA	上海	中国
XIAN	SIA	西安	中国
SINGAPORE	SIN	新加坡	新加坡
BERLIN	SXF	柏林	德国
SYDNEY	SYD	悉尼	澳大利亚
SANYA	SYX	三亚	中国

附录C 国内主要城市航空三字代码及机场

Codes of Cities in China

国内(大陆)主要城市航空三字代码及机场

省份	城市	城市代码	机场名称	省份	城市	城市代码	机场名称
海南省	海口	HAK	美兰国际机场	北京市	北京	PEK	首都国际机场
	三亚	SYX	凤凰国际机场		北京南苑	NAY	北京南苑机场
广东省	广州	CAN	白云国际机场	浙江省	杭州	HGH	萧山国际机场
	珠海	ZUH	金湾机场		温州	WNZ	龙湾国际机场
	深圳	SZX	宝安国际机场		宁波	NGB	栎社国际机场
	汕头	SWA	外砂机场		义乌	YIW	义乌机场
	梅州	MXZ	梅县机场		舟山	HSN	舟山普陀山机场
	湛江	ZHA	湛江机场		台州	HYN	黄岩路桥机场
	韶关	HSC	韶关机场		衢州	JUZ	衢州机场
	兴宁	XIN	兴城机场	江苏省	南京	NKG	禄口国际机场
广西壮族自治区	南宁	NNG	吴圩机场		连云港	LYG	白塔埠机场
	桂林	KWL	两江国际机场		南通	NTG	兴东机场
	百色	AEB	百色机场		常州	CZX	奔牛机场
	柳州	LZH	白莲机场		徐州	XUZ	观音机场
	梧州	WUZ	长洲岛机场		盐城	YNZ	南洋机场
	北海	BHY	福成机场		无锡	WUX	硕放机场
湖南省	长沙	CSX	黄花国际机场	山东省	济南	TNA	遥墙机场
	张家界	DYG	荷花机场		威海	WEH	文登大水泊机场
	常德	CGD	桃花源机场		青岛	TAO	流亭机场
	衡阳	HNY	南岳机场		烟台	YNT	莱山机场
	芷江	HJJ	芷江机场		济宁	JNG	济宁机场
	永州	LLF	零陵机场		潍坊	WEF	潍坊机场
重庆市	重庆	CKG	江北机场		东营	DOY	东营机场
	万州	WXN	万州机场				

国内(大陆)主要城市航空三字代码及机场

省份	城市	城市代码	机场名称	省份	城市	城市代码	机场名称
湖北省	武汉	WUH	天河机场	江西省	南昌	KHN	昌北机场
	宜昌	YIH	三峡机场		景德镇	JDZ	罗家机场
	襄阳	XFN	刘集机场		九江	JIU	庐山机场
	荆州	SHS	荆州沙市机场		井冈山	JGS	井冈山机场
	恩施	ENH	恩施机场		赣州	KOW	黄金机场
福建省	福州	FOC	长乐国际机场	贵州省	贵阳	KWE	龙洞堡国际机场
	厦门	XMN	高崎国际机场		遵义	ZYI	遵义新舟机场
	南平	WUS	武夷山机场		安顺	AVA	黄果树机场
	泉州	JJN	泉州晋江机场		铜仁	TEN	铜仁凤凰机场
					兴义	ACX	兴义机场
黑龙江	哈尔滨	HRB	太平国际机场	安徽省	合肥	HFE	新桥国际机场
	齐齐哈尔	NDG	三家子机场		黄山	TXN	屯溪国际机场
	牡丹江	MDG	海浪机场		阜阳	FUG	阜阳西关机场
	满洲里	NZH	呼伦贝尔满洲里西郊机场		安庆	AQG	天柱山机场
	佳木斯	JMU	佳木斯机场	河南省	郑州	CGO	新郑机场
	黑河	HEK	黑河机场		洛阳	LYA	洛阳机场
四川省	成都	CTU	双流国际机场		南阳	NNY	姜营机场
	泸州	LZO	泸州机场		安阳	AYN	安阳北郊机场
	宜宾	YBP	莱坝机场	河北省	石家庄	SJW	正定机场
	绵阳	MIG	南郊机场		秦皇岛	SHP	山海关机场
	九寨沟	JZH	黄龙机场	陕西省	西安	XIY	咸阳国际机场
	攀枝花	PZI	保安营机场		延安	ENY	延安二十里铺机场
	达州	DAX	河市机场		安康	AKA	安康机场
	西昌市	XTC	青山机场		榆林	UYN	榆阳机场
	南充	NAO	高坪机场		汉中	HZG	汉中城固机场
	广元	GYS	盘龙机场				

续表

国内(大陆)主要城市航空三字代码及机场

省份	城市	城市代码	机场名称	省份	城市	城市代码	机场名称
上海市	上海	PVG	浦东国际机场	天津市	天津	TSN	滨海国际机场
		SHA	虹桥机场	甘肃省	兰州	LHW	中川机场
吉林省	长春	CGQ	龙嘉机场		敦煌	DNH	敦煌机场
	吉林	JIL	二台子机场		嘉峪关	JGN	嘉峪关机场
	延吉	YNJ	朝阳川机场		酒泉	CHW	酒泉机场
山西省	太原	TYN	武宿机场		庆阳	IQN	庆阳机场
	大同	DAT	云冈机场	云南省	昆明	KMG	长水机场
	长治	CIH	王村机场		丽江	LJG	三义机场
新疆维吾尔自治区	乌鲁木齐	URC	地窝堡机场		西双版纳	JHG	嘎洒机场
	喀什	KHG	喀什机场		大理	DLU	大理机场
	伊宁	YIN	伊宁机场		普洱	SYM	思茅机场
	库尔勒	KRL	库尔勒机场		保山	BSD	保山机场
	阿克苏	AKU	阿克苏机场		临沧	LNJ	临沧机场
	和田	HTN	和田机场		昭通	ZAT	昭通机场
	阿勒泰	AAT	阿勒泰机场	内蒙古自治区	呼和浩特	HET	050白塔机场
	哈密	HMI	哈密机场		包头	BAC	包头机场
辽宁省	沈阳	SHE	桃仙国际机场		锡林浩特	XIL	锡林浩特机场
	大连	DLC	周水子机场		乌兰浩特	HLH	乌兰浩特机场
	丹东	DDG	浪头机场		海拉尔	HLD	海拉尔机场
	鞍山	AOG	鞍山机场		乌海	WUA	乌海机场
青海省	西宁	XNN	曹家堡机场		赤峰	CIF	玉龙机场
	格尔木	GOQ	格尔木机场		通辽	TGO	通辽机场
宁夏回族自治区	银川	INC	河东机场	西藏自治区	拉萨	LXA	拉萨贡嘎国际机场

附录 D 机上特殊餐食及代码

特餐四字代码	英文全称	中文全称	中文注解
AVML	Vegetarian Asian(hindu)Meal	亚洲素餐	亚洲素餐通常由来自南亚次大陆的旅客选择。通常是亚洲生产的蔬菜
BBML	Baby Meal	婴儿餐	含肉类、蔬菜或水果类,质地多为糊状
BLML	Bland Meal	清淡餐	菜肴包括低脂肪和低纤维食物,避免油炸食物、黑胡椒、含气植物、芥末、咸菜、大蒜、坚果和含咖啡因或酒精的饮料。适合有胃肠疾病的旅客进食
CHML	Child Meal	儿童餐	菜肴含有儿童喜欢的食物,如汉蛋、薯条等。避免过咸过甜食品
DBML	Diabetic Meal	糖尿病餐	菜肴是无糖、低盐食物,适合糖尿病人食用。不含有任何种类的糖
FPML	Fruit Platter Meal	水果餐	菜肴只包括水果。包括新鲜水果、糖渍水果和水果甜品
GFML	Gluten Free Meal	无麸质餐	菜肴是为麸质过敏和不耐的客人准备的。(麸质是存在于小麦、大麦、燕麦、黑麦等中的蛋白质)面包、汁类、奶油蛋汤、蛋糕、巧克力、饼干、谷物及其制品被严禁使用
HNML	Hindu Meal	印度教餐	不包括牛肉或猪肉,但包括羊肉、家禽,其他肉类、鱼和牛奶制品专为少数可吃肉或鱼的印度旅客准备
KSML	Kosher Meal	犹太教餐	一切准备按犹太饮食习惯,餐食干净,并购自有信誉的制造商(一般需提前48小时申请)
LCML	Low Calorie Meal	低卡路里餐	菜肴包括瘦肉、低脂肪奶制品和高纤维食物。糖、奶油、汁类、蛋黄酱、脂肪食品被禁止使用
LFML	Low Fat Meal	低脂肪餐/低胆固醇餐	菜肴适合需要减少脂肪摄入量的客人食用。不含油炸食品、肥肉、奶制品、加工食品、浓汁、内脏、带壳水产品、蛋黄和焙烤制品

143

续表

特餐四字代码	英文全称	中文全称	中文注解
LSML	Low Salt Meal	低盐餐	菜肴中的盐有一定的控制量,是为患有高血压、闭尿症和肾病的乘客准备的。食品不含盐、蒜盐、谷氨酸钠、苏打、腌渍咸菜、罐头肉和鱼、奶油、芝士、贝壳类、土豆泥、肉汁类、鸡粉、面包、罐头蔬菜
MOML	Moslem Meal	穆斯林餐(清真餐)	菜肴不含有猪肉、重肉、火腿肠类、动物油脂或酒精及无鳞鱼类、鳗鱼和甲鱼,所有的家禽和动物在被宰杀和烹饪时需要按照伊斯兰教的有关规定
NLML	No Lactose Meal	无乳糖餐	餐肴不包括乳糖及奶类制品,亦没有任何相关材料,不含奶酪奶制品、酸奶、黄油、人造肉制品、蛋糕及饼干、奶油类甜品、布丁、土豆泥、太妃糖、巧克力和奶油
RVML	Vegetarian Raw Meal	生蔬菜餐	餐食仅以水果及蔬菜为原料。不含有任何动物蛋白原料
SFML	Seafood Meal	海鲜餐	专为喜欢海鲜的旅客定制。菜肴包括一种或多种海鲜。不含肉类制品
VGML	Vegetarian Vegan Meal	纯素餐	纯素餐也被称为"Vegan Meal"。餐食中不能含有任何动物或动物制品。菜肴不包括肉、鱼或奶制品、鸡蛋、奶酪及相关制品,可食用人造黄油
VJML	Vegetarian Jain Meal	耆那教餐	专为耆那教徒提供,是严格的餐食,用亚洲方法烹制。无任何根类植物如洋葱、姜、大蒜、胡萝卜等,无任何动物制品
VLML	Vegetarian Lacto-ovo Meal	西式素食餐	菜肴不包括肉或海鲜及其制品,但包括日常的黄油、奶酪、牛奶和鸡蛋
VOML	Vegetarian Oriental Meal	东方素食餐	按中式或东方的烹饪方法制作。不带有肉、鱼或野味、奶制品或任何生长在地下的根茎类蔬菜,如生姜、大蒜、洋葱、大葱等

教学支持说明

高等职业学校"十四五"规划民航服务类系列教材系华中科技大学出版社"十四五"期间重点教材。

为了改善教学效果，提高教材的使用效率，满足高校授课教师的教学需求，本套教材备有与纸质教材配套的参考答案、教学课件（PPT电子教案）和拓展资源（案例库、习题库等）。

为保证本教学课件及相关教学资料仅为教材使用者所用，我们将向使用本套教材的高校授课教师免费赠送教学课件或相关教学资料，烦请授课教师通过电话、邮件或加入旅游专家俱乐部QQ群等方式与我们联系，获取"电子资源申请表"文档，准确填写后发给我们，我们的联系方式如下：

地址：湖北省武汉市东湖新技术开发区华工科技园华工园六路

邮编：430223

电话：027-81321911

传真：027-81321917

E-mail：lyzjjlb@163.com

民航专家俱乐部QQ群号：799420527

民航专家俱乐部QQ群二维码：

扫一扫二维码，加入群聊。

电子资源申请表

填表时间：_____年____月____日

1. 以下内容请教师按实际情况填写，★为必填项。
2. 相关内容可以酌情调整提交。

★姓名		★性别	□男 □女	出生年月		★职务	
						★职称	□教授 □副教授 □讲师 □助教

★学校		★院/系	
★教研室		★专业	
★办公电话		家庭电话		★移动电话	
★E-mail（请填写清晰）				★QQ号/微信号	
★联系地址				★邮编	

★现在主授课程情况	学生人数	教材所属出版社	教材满意度
课程一			□满意 □一般 □不满意
课程二			□满意 □一般 □不满意
课程三			□满意 □一般 □不满意
其 他			□满意 □一般 □不满意

教 材 出 版 信 息						
方向一		□准备写	□写作中	□已成稿	□已出版待修订	□有讲义
方向二		□准备写	□写作中	□已成稿	□已出版待修订	□有讲义
方向三		□准备写	□写作中	□已成稿	□已出版待修订	□有讲义

请教师认真填写表格下列内容，提供索取课件配套教材的相关信息，我社将根据每位教师填表信息的完整性、授课情况与索取课件的相关性，以及教材使用的情况赠送教材的配套课件及相关教学资源。

ISBN(书号)	书名	作者	索取课件简要说明	学生人数（如选作教材）
			□教学 □参考	
			□教学 □参考	

★您对与课件配套的纸质教材的意见和建议，希望提供哪些配套教学资源：